NATIONAL HISTORIC
MECHANICAL ENGINEERING LANDMARK

HART - PARR TRACTOR
1903

THIS WAS THE FIRST COMMERCIALLY SUCCESSFUL FARM TRACTOR IN THE WORLD POWERED BY AN INTERNAL-COMBUSTION ENGINE. IT WAS INVENTED AND BUILT BY CHARLES W. HART AND CHARLES H. PARR IN CHARLES CITY, IOWA, AS THEIR MODEL 3, FOLLOWING TWO PROTOTYPE VERSIONS.

GASOLINE AND KEROSENE TRACTORS SUCCESSFULLY COMPETED IN THE MIDWEST WITH STEAM TRACTORS FOR BOTH DRAWBAR AND BELT WORK AS THEY PRESENTED LESS FIRE DANGER, THEY DID NOT REQUIRE LARGE VOLUMES OF WATER, AND THE LIQUID FUEL WAS MORE READILY AVAILABLE AND EASIER TO HANDLE.

 THE AMERICAN SOCIETY OF MECHANICAL ENGINEERS - 1996

OLIVER
Farm Tractors

T. Herbert Morrell & Jeff Hackett

Motorbooks International
Publishers & Wholesalers

Dedication

I dedicate this book to my wife, Blanche S. Morrell, who has been very supportive during my entire professional career. She has assisted in the editing of this book, provided many good suggestions, and helped me in numerous other ways.

T. Herbert Morrell
Owatonna, Minnesota
June, 1996

First published in 1997 by Motorbooks International Publishers & Wholesalers, 729 Prospect Avenue, PO Box 1, Osceola, WI 54020-0001 USA

Motorbooks International books are also available at discounts in bulk quantity for industrial or sales-promotional use. For details write to Special Sales Manager at the Publisher's address

Library of Congress Cataloging-in-Publication Data

Morrell, T. Herbert.
    Oliver Farm tractors / T. Herbert Morrell & Jeff Hackett.
      p. cm.
    Includes Index.
    ISBN 0-7603-0356-8 (alk. paper)
      1. Oliver tractors--History. 2. Oliver Corporation--History. I. Hackett, Jeff. II. Title.
      TL233.6.043M67   1997
      629.225'2--dc21   97-13151

On the front cover: The first of the Oliver Fleetline tractors, the Model 66, 77, and 88, were dubbed the "three beauties" in Oliver's ad campaign for the new machines. The cover photograph shows off these three tractors, a 1950 Row Crop 66, 1953 Row Crop 77 Diesel, and 1949 Row Crop 88. Owned by Bobby Quigley

On the frontispiece: The Charles City Hart-Parr Model 30-60 tractor was declared a National Historic Mechanical Engineering Landmark on May 18, 1996, because it was the first commercially successful gasoline-powered tractor.

On the title page: A 1961 Model 660 with adjustable wide front axle. The Model 660 was the redesign of the Super 66, and was built from 1959 to 1964. Owned by Bill Meeker

On the back cover: A 1955 Super 66. The Super series followed the Fleetline tractors. The new line featured more power and features and was introduced in 1954. Production of the Super 66 ran until 1958. Owned by Bill Meeker

Text by T. Herbert Morrell
Photography by Jeff Hackett

Editor: Lee Klancher
Designer: Katie Finney

Printed in China through World Print, Ltd.

Contents

ACKNOWLEDGMENTS

I wish to thank those who helped me with this book. Members of the Hart-Parr/Oliver Collectors Association encouraged me to write this book and they provided much information. Bob Tallman and Sherry Schaefer have been extremely helpful. Special thanks go to the Oliver and Hart-Parr collectors who permitted photos of their tractors to be included in the book.

A lot of people provided photos and historical information, including Leland (Skip) Hartwell, Kurt Aumann, Mary Ann Townsend of the Floyd County Historical Society in Charles City, Iowa, and my brother-in-law Harold W. Snyder. Keith L. (Punch) Pfundstein sent information and photos of Charles F. Kettering and his participation in the XO-121 research project. Glenn B. Bazen provided photographs of Lull Engineering's uses of Oliver tractors. Doug Strawser provided information on the number of tractors and combines sold to Russia in the 1930s, and Edna Ladd gave some insight into Oliver's circumstances at that time. Samuel W. White Jr. has been interested in the book from the beginning and graciously agreed to write the foreword.

I am grateful to Sherry Schaefer, Doug Strawser, Guy Fay, and Lorry Dunning for reviewing the final manuscript and, especially, to our editor, Lee Klancher, who was enthusiastic about the project and guided us every step of the way.

Because of her desktop publishing experience, my daughter Judy Lumb was very helpful and spent many hours refining and editing the text. My wife, Blanche, son, Dennis Morrell, and daughter Becky Schmitz have all been supportive, and they encouraged me to write this book.

T. Herbert Morrell
Owatonna, Minnesota
June, 1996

As a photographer, I meet many people from all walks of life. Being introduced to Herb Morrell and subsequently meeting and talking to many of the Oliver tractor collectors and their families, I have come to know some of the nicest people you could ever encounter. I feel honored to be associated with Herb, his wife, Blanche, and his daughter, Judy. To have sat with Herb discussing the Oliver book project and Oliver in general is a time I will always remember.

As an outsider looking in, Bob Tallman provided me with history and stories about Oliver that could not be found anywhere else. I want to thank Wayne Wiltse and Mary Ann Townsend of the Floyd County Historical Society in Charles City, Iowa, Sherry Schaefer, and all of the Oliver tractor owners for opening their homes and barns and allowing me to photograph these beautiful machines: Jim Kline; Bill Meeker and his dog; Everett Jensen; George Elliot; Kenny J. Grimm and his dad Hilbert; Albert "Sparky" Duroe; Robert Duncan and his son; Bobby Quigley and his son; Richard Hollinger and his sons; and Karl Snider and Steve Weigel.

I would like to thank my wife, Lauren and son, Wyatt (who loves his Oliver toys) for the time to travel and complete this project.

Jeff Hackett
Bridgeport, Connecticut
March, 1997

FOREWORD

I am honored to be asked to write a foreword for this most remarkable and detailed book on the accomplishments of the Oliver Corporation. Especially noteworthy are the author's personal contributions to the progress of Oliver's work and its recognition among the major U.S. and foreign tractor manufacturers.

Tractors are the backbone of a full-line agricultural machinery manufacturer. The farming (and later industrial) customer, the sales and service personnel in the Oliver dealer network, the loyal and dedicated Oliver employees in the plants, branches, and overseas all freely expressed their admiration for the high quality, innovative features, productivity, and long life of Oliver tractors.

My career with Oliver started at the South Bend, Indiana, plant before I finished graduate school and resumed after World War II. I served as Oliver president from 1960 to 1970 after White Motor Corporation purchased the Oliver Corporation in 1960. From my vantage point as chief executive officer in the Chicago office and my constant travels to visit our branches, dealers, and competitors, I witnessed firsthand the high regard accorded Oliver's products and the special praise reserved for the Charles City plant engineers and their plant personnel. What a joy it was to see the ready acceptance of the many forward-looking firsts and competitive innovations that Herb Morrell and his staff brought to the Oliver Corporation.

I enjoyed a most pleasant personal and professional relationship with Herb Morrell. I supported his programs, congratulated his dedicated staff, heralded his designs, and took the lead in seeking recognition for Oliver products—their features, productivity, cost efficiency, operator-friendliness, and safety. Readers of this book will stand in awe and admiration of the author's accomplishments, many of which came during his distinguished service as chief engineer.

I was grateful to Herb for bringing forth the Three Beauties—the Fleetline 66, 77, and 88—for opening the diesel engine era, and for his involvement in developing the Super 55, the 1800, the 1900, and all the others that followed.

Sam White Jr. (right), president of Oliver Corporation from 1960 to 1970, is shown with George Bird (left), plant manager of Oliver's Charles City Plant from 1944 to 1961.

I can truthfully state that Oliver Corporation, as a proud subsidiary of White Motor Corporation during my term, was the most profitable and shareholder-appreciated White Motor operation. This book tells, in part, how this was accomplished and how Oliver earned its coveted product leadership. I thank Herb for writing this book on behalf of all the Oliver personnel, dealers, suppliers, and loyal customers everywhere. He is a "10" in my book.

Sam W. White Jr.

PREFACE

It was a special privilege to have been a part of agriculture and agribusiness through most of the 20th century. Our main goals were to keep the cost of food as low as possible and to reach the areas of the world where people were hungry.

Growing up on a farm in Kansas, I was not happy with the quality and function of farm equipment in the 1920s and 1930s. It seemed necessary to make modifications to each piece of equipment. For example, on our Farmall tractor, we added steps and other ways a driver could rest his feet to reduce body fatigue.

Other good examples of changes that were needed were the two McCormick-Deering Reapers our family purchased from the last production run. The first Reaper was assembled with soft steel bolts and capscrews. The bolts and capscrews soon wore down, became loose, and failed. The lock washers soon broke as well. Another shortcoming was that the bearings for the main shafts were made of cast iron. This combination of a steel shaft running in a cast-iron bearing is not the best.

We purchased the second unit unassembled and assembled it on our farm. In all of those places where we had experienced problems, we made modifications to correct the problems. We used heat-treated bolts and capscrews and left out the lock washers, adding a second nut instead. The first nut was tightened to nearly the maximum strength of the heat-treated bolt. The second nut was tightened securely to the first nut, which became a locknut. We removed the cast-iron bearings, aligned the shafts, and poured babbit material in the place of the cast-iron. This second unit lasted for thousands of hours cutting flax in eastern Kansas.

The Great Depression of the early 1930s caused many changes in my life. My high school studies were all commercial because I was planning to be a farmer. I graduated in May 1934 and went into partnership on the farm with my father and youngest brother. The next two years were devastating ones for me on the farm. There were 10 days in July when the temperature never got below 100 degrees F, day or night. There had been little rain all year. Farmers were selling most of their livestock because of the water shortage.

My brother-in-law, George Weatherbie, was in the trucking business, hauling grain to market and livestock to the Kansas City Stockyards. He contracted to haul many loads of livestock and that kept him busy from Sunday noon to Wednesday morning. George drove the truck when it was loaded and I slept in the truck's cab. Then I drove the empty truck while George slept.

Because there had been a poor potato crop in our area, we drove to the Kansas River area near Lawrence where potatoes were available for 10 cents per bushel if we picked up the potatoes. We cleaned the truck, lined the bed with tar paper, and took a load of potatoes home to sell.

As I was picking up potatoes, I could see on a nearby hill the beautiful University of Kansas buildings of native stone and red tile roofs. I asked George if we could stop by the engineering department. I changed into a pair of clean overalls and made the visit. Professor Jones, acting dean of engineering, was supportive of my desire to get an engineering degree and my goal of designing better farm equipment. He directed me to Mrs. Palmer, who was in charge of employment for students. She assured me that I could find employment through the requests that came to her. I eventually graduated with a bachelor of science degree in mechanical engineering, with majors in design and powerplant.

When I graduated in 1941, the farm equipment companies were not hiring young engineers, so I accepted an offer from DuPont to design factory machinery in Wilmington, Delaware. I was directed instead to Remington Arms Company, a division of DuPont, in Bridgeport, Connecticut, where I became an ammunition engineer. I was frozen to my job for the war effort until mid-1944. By this time, food and farm equipment were the top national priority, so I decided to pursue my interest in farm machinery engineering. I had many interviews and accepted a position as design engineer at the Oliver Farm Equipment Company in Charles City,

Iowa. In 1950, I was promoted to assistant chief engineer and then to chief engineer in 1951, a position I held until 1965 when I moved to the Chicago office as coordinator of outside products. I continued to be involved as a consultant in further developments and improvements of the Fleetline tractors until 1970.

When I was first asked by members of the Hart-Parr/Oliver Collectors Association to write this book, I declined. But they said that the development of the famous Fleetline 66, 77, and 88 tractors is an important story, and since Oliver is no longer a company, I should write a book about it because I know more details than anyone else alive at that time.

The famous Oliver Fleetline tractors established a new standard for the industry. They were practical and economical diesel tractors with many innovations such as independent power take-off, easy-riding seat, and hydraulics controlled by electrical circuits. This book tells the story of the development of the Fleetline 66, 77, and 88 and their successors. It is a look behind the scenes at the people involved, the design criteria, the engineering considerations, the testing, and the problems, along with their solutions.

T. Herbert Morrell
June 1996

AUTHOR BIOGRAPHY
T. HERBERT MORRELL
July 31, 1916–October 2, 1996

T. Herbert Morrell was born and raised on a farm near Blue Mound, Kansas. In addition to farming, his family built silos, water reservoirs, barns, and other farm buildings. In the mid-1920s they also maintained natural gas wells in the area. He went to a country grade school, attended high school in Blue Mound, and earned a bachelor of science degree in mechanical engineering from the University of Kansas in 1941. His first position was as an ammunition engineer for Remington Arms Company in Bridgeport, Connecticut, during World War II. In 1944, he began working for Oliver Farm Equipment Company in Charles City, Iowa, as a design engineer. He was promoted to assistant chief engineer in 1950, and promoted to chief engineer in 1951. His title changed to senior chief engineer in 1963, when crawler tractors became part of his domain.

During his time with Oliver's engineering department, Morrell played key roles in the development of several innovative Oliver products and features, including the development of the Fleetline tractors and testing with the XO-121 experimental tractor.

From 1965 to 1970, Morrell was coordinator of outside products at Oliver's corporate headquarters in Chicago. He was vice president of engineering with Owatonna Manufacturing Company until 1977, when he became a management consultant for design engineering and safety. Morrell served as an expert witness in approximately 150 product liability lawsuits. A member of the Society of Automotive Engineers (SAE) and a Fellow (Distinguished Member) of the American Society of Agricultural Engineers (ASAE), he was especially interested in the safety of agricultural equipment and served for many years on the safety standards committees of the SAE, ASAE, and the American National Standards Institute. Even though his health was declining as he wrote this book, he worked hard to finish it. The manuscript was completed on September 29, 1996, and he died three days later.

T. Herbert Morrell (center) seated in the engineering department while selecting Timken tapered bearings in 1961 with Ernie Williamson (left) of the Oliver purchasing department and Bob Morgan (right) of Timken Bearing. *C. J. Gibbs*

COMPANY HISTORY

The Oliver Company roots can be traced back to Hart-Parr, a company founded by Charles W. Hart and Charles Parr. Hart was born in Charles City, Iowa, in 1872. He attended Iowa State University at Ames for a year, then transferred to the University of Wisconsin at Madison. Charles Parr was born March 18, 1868, on a farm near Dodgeville, Wisconsin. He met his future partner, Charles W. Hart, at the University of Wisconsin. In 1895, while still students at the university, Hart and Parr started experimental work on gasoline engines. Two years later, April 29, 1897, the two aspiring engineers formed the Hart-Parr Company in Madison, but they had difficulty getting sufficient financial backing there. Hart's father and Charles City bankers C. D. and A. E. Ellis persuaded them to move the Hart-Parr Company to Hart's hometown.

The company moved to Charles City in 1901 and was reorganized June 12, 1901. Construction of the Charles City plant began on July 5, 1901, and was completed, along with the transfer from Madison, on December 25, 1901. As the partnership evolved, it became apparent that Hart was the idea man while Parr used his skills as an engineer to develop Hart's ideas and make the drawings.

Both Hart and Parr were civic-minded and active in Charles City affairs. For example, J. E. Waggoner, an Iowa State University graduate in mechanical engineering, had a special interest in internal combustion engines. But when he was hired to work in the

HART-PARR
FOUNDERS OF THE TRACTOR INDUSTRY

Hart-Parr engineering department, no tractor design assignments were available. Instead, he was assigned the job of designing a suspension foot bridge over the Cedar River to connect the main residential district of Charles City with the athletic fields across the river. The foot bridge is still in use and was placed on the National Register of Historic Places in 1989.

During World War I, Hart-Parr got an order to make artillery shells for the U.S. Army. But raw steel was in such short supply that the company tooled up to make steel. It was 1917, nearly the end of the war, before they had assembled the tools, machined all the parts, and were ready for production. The government then canceled the contract because they had already stockpiled enough artillery for the rest of the war, leaving the Hart-Parr Company in a financial strain.

Hart left Hart-Parr that same year after a conflict with the Charles City bankers C. D. and A. E. Ellis. He moved to Montana where he established the Hart Refinery and registered patent number 1,458,936 on June 19, 1923, for a "method of harvesting grain." His invention was a header barge that cut and collected the heads of the grain crop. The Hart Refinery in Hedgesville, Montana, supplied gasoline and other petroleum products to approximately 10 filling stations that he owned. Later, with a partner, Hart set up a larger refinery in Missoula, Montana, and continued in the oil refinery business until he died on March

Hart-Parr built its first tractor in the winter and spring of 1902. Founded by Charles Hart and Charles Parr, the company was the first to produce a commercially successful tractor. This model, the Hart-Parr 20-40, was built from 1911 to 1914.

ABOVE: The Hart-Parr 16-30 shown on the cover of this brochure was built from 1924 to 1926. *Floyd County Historical Society*

Charles W. Hart (1872–1937) was born in Charles City, Iowa. He and Charles Parr formed a partnership while still students at the University of Wisconsin. They will be remembered as the inventors of the first successful commercially produced agricultural tractor. Hart was the idea man of the two partners and left Hart-Parr in 1917 for a career in the oil refinery business in Montana. *Floyd County Historical Society*

Charles H. Parr (1868–1941) was born near Dodgeville, Wisconsin. He and Charles Hart produced the first commercially successful tractor. Parr was the detail man, the engineer who developed the detailed plans for their inventions. Except for one year as chief engineer of the Elgin Street Sweeper Company in Elgin, Illinois, Parr spent his entire career with Hart-Parr and its successor, Oliver Farm Equipment Company. *Floyd County Historical Society*

24, 1937. He is buried in Riverside Cemetery in Charles City. The eulogy was read by his former partner, Charlie Parr.

Parr remained with Hart-Parr and the new company, Oliver Farm Equipment Company, except for a short stint in 1923–24 when he worked as chief engineer of the Elgin Street Sweeper Company in Elgin, Illinois. He died in June 1941 and is also buried in Riverside Cemetery.

The Hart-Parr Company started producing stationary engines in a small brick building. Approximately 305 stationary engines were built from 1898 to 1904. The more powerful two- and four-cylinder engines were manufactured for stationary use during 1921 to 1929.

Once in the early 1950s, I was taking Alva Phelps, president of Oliver Corporation at that time, and some other Oliver executives on a tour of the Charles City tractor plant. We saw a strange part being machined and asked what it was. The blueprint called it a stationary engine casting, which was a cylinder for a stationary engine that had not been manufactured since 1904. They were being machined to fill a repair order for 50 parts to be shipped to Australia!

While the stationary engines were powerful and durable, farmers needed their machinery to move through the fields. So Hart and Parr, while they were producing their stationary engines, were also designing moveable machines they called gasoline traction engines. The first, Hart-Parr No. 1, was manufactured in 1902 and was sold to an Iowa farmer who used it for several years. Hart-Parr No. 2 was built in 1902 and sold in 1903. Hart-Parr No. 3, built in 1903, was used by the original owner for 17 years and is now in the Agricultural Collection of the National Museum of American History at the Smithsonian Institution in Washington, D. C. As of Spring 1997, it was on display at Lakefarm Park in Kirkland, Ohio.

Hart-Parr gasoline traction engine production took off in 1903 with 14 Model 17-30s and 21 Model 22-40s. The first number indicates the rated drawbar horsepower (17 or 22) and the second is the rated belt horsepower (30 or 40). These models remained in production until 1906. In 1906 the valve gearing was changed from pushrod type to rotary valve, and the tractors were re-rated 22-45 in 1908. The Model 30-60 was produced from 1911 to 1918 and became nicknamed "Old Reliable." A detailed listing of all tractors manufactured by Hart-Parr and its successors is given in Appendix A.

In 1964 an Old Reliable built in 1913 was acquired by the Oliver Management Club. They gained permission to construct a steel and Plexiglas display shelter on the Floyd County courthouse lawn

where it stood until the Floyd County Historical Society was organized. The Floyd County Museum in Charles City now has three Hart-Parr tractors that were manufactured before 1920, the Old Reliable 30-60, a Hart-Parr 20-40, and a Little Red Devil 15-22. The latter two were purchased in the summer of 1996 after a "Bring the Tractors Home" fund drive.

It was Hart-Parr's sales manager, W. H. Williams, who thought the name "gasoline traction engine" was too long and shortened it to "tractor." Williams was not the first to use the term. It had been used before by G.H. Edwards of Chicago in patent number 425,000, issued in 1870. But this variation of a steam engine was never produced commercially, so the term never caught on. Williams' use of the term did catch on, however, and has since become an accepted word in the English language.

Hart-Parr Innovations

Hart-Parr was the first to manufacture a practical internal combustion tractor engine. This was a better alternative to steam power on the farm because the large quantities of water and fuel required made steam expensive. Hart-Parr tractors required only low-cost liquid fuels. This innovation started a new tractor trend and the Charles City Hart-Parr plant became the first successful tractor plant.

Not only were Hart-Parr tractors the first of their kind, but the company continued in that tradition of innovation with many creative ideas through the years. Most Hart-Parr tractor engines could burn low-grade, low-cost fuels, such as kerosene or distillate. The engine was started on gasoline and, after it was warm, could be switched to lower grade fuel. In order to ignite the fuel when the engine was idling, the lower grade fuel was heated by shunting it around the exhaust manifold. Under full-load conditions, the

low-grade fuel was not shunted because the engine heat was great enough to keep the fuel warm to assist the ignition. Some of these engines had water injection for antiknock when burning kerosene. This reduced the cost of operation to half since gasoline was quite expensive.

Hart-Parr power ratings were quite conservative. For example, the 18-36 Model developed 32.25 horsepower on the drawbar and 42.85 on the belt. Such a rating provided surplus power of 79 percent and 19 percent, respectively. The tractor engine speed was governed to increase pulling power at lower than maximum engine speed, which allowed the tractor to carry the heavier drawbar loads through the tough spots.

The company boasted about having enough power for large threshers and combines. Hart-Parr tractors were successful in the large wheat fields of USA, Canada, Australia, New Zealand, South America, Africa, and Asia. Smaller tractors, such as the 12-24 Model, were popular in France, Italy, Hungary, and other areas of Europe. So, Hart-Parr became the first American tractor company with substantial foreign business.

Hart-Parr developed the first:
- Oil-cooled engine, which had advantages because the oil would not freeze in cold weather and damage the engine.
- Valve-in-head engine, which was more efficient and had a longer life than the L-head engines with the valves in the crankcase. The valve-in-head engine was also easier to service and provided better fuel economy.
- Force-fed lubrication, which provided more adequate and continuous engine lubrication.
- Multi-speed transmission, which added to the versatility of tractors so they could do more agricultural functions that had been done by horses. The transmission and final drive gears were over-designed, resulting in good reliability and long life.

Hart-Parr offered quite a selection of wheels for angle, spade, and spike lugs. In fact, the 12-24, 18-36, and 28-50 models were offered with solid rubber treads on the front and rear wheels. Rubber treads were offered for use where conventional steel wheels and lugs were not permitted or were not practical.

Hart-Parr manufactured stationary power units in Madison, Wisconsin, and continued in Charles City, Iowa. These units were produced from 1897 to 1904. Mike Shanks owns this restored stationary engine and lives on a farm near Nora Springs, Iowa, which was originally purchased by his grandfather, Winfield Hart, who was Charles Hart's brother. It is believed this farm was used by Hart-Parr for experimental purposes. *Floyd County Historical Society*

HART-PARR
FOUNDERS OF THE TRACTOR INDUSTRY

Hart-Parr began a tradition of innovation that was continued by the Oliver Corporation. Hart-Parr is even responsible for the current use of the word "tractor" in our language. The first units were called "gasoline traction engines," but that seemed too unwieldy, so the Hart-Parr sales department shortened it to "tractor." *Floyd County Historical Society*

The independent power take-off (PTO) was first introduced on the Hart-Parr 18-36 in 1928. But it was way ahead of its time and there was not much interest in this early innovation. The implements, with the exception of the combines, did not require much power so that the advantage of the independent PTO was not apparent. The independent PTO did, however, become a very important part of the development of the famous Oliver Fleetline tractors introduced in the late 1940s.

In 1928, prior to rubber tires on tractors, Oliver Chilled Plow developed the Tip Toe rear wheels. The theory behind this development was for the rear wheels to penetrate the loose soil on top of the ground into more firm soil for traction. This gave the rear wheels adequate traction without compacting the topsoil. The Tip Toe rear wheels were very popular on the Oliver Hart-Parr tractors and the Row Crop 70, until rubber tires were introduced in the mid-1930s.

A railway was needed to connect the Hart-Parr plant in Charles City with the Illinois Central and Rock Island railways. So, to transport the tractors, the Charles City Western Railway was organized in 1910. It was initially capitalized at $300,000. The directors were C. W. Hart, C. H. Parr, A. E. Ellis, C. D. Ellis, E. M. Sherman, N. Frudden, and F. W. Fisher. During the first directors' meeting, C. W. Hart was elected president of the board. The Charles City Western Railway originally ran from Charles City to the nearby Iowa towns of Rockford, Marble Rock, and Greene. Later, it was extended to Colwell, Iowa.

Thede Rowley was my next-door neighbor when I first moved to Charles City in 1944. He had retired after spending most of his life working for Hart-Parr/Oliver and had many interesting stories to tell. I will always remember one story he told. During his last few years at Oliver, Mr. Parr was referred to as the "Old Man." The plant had a high-capacity jack used for lifting big machines that also was referred to as the Old Man. One day, Thede and others were repairing some factory machinery and a new employee was asked to get the "Old Man" since it was needed to lift a machine. He came back with Mr. Parr instead of the big jack.

C. E. Frudden was chief engineer of Hart-Parr for many years until about 1920, when he left to work for Parret Tractor. A few years after, he left Parret to become chief engineer or director of engineering at Allis Chalmers. It was my pleasure to visit with C. E. Frudden at a meeting of the Society of Automotive Engineers in Milwaukee, Wisconsin, after I became chief engineer of Oliver in October 1951. Our conversation centered on current industry problems and standards.

A. H. Witt was another important figure in the early Hart-Parr organization. Shortly after he was employed by Hart-Parr, he entered the accounting department. In September 1917, he was made assistant secretary and assistant treasurer. He became secretary in July 1920 and continued as assistant treasurer. He held this position until he became comptroller of the Oliver Farm Equipment Company following the merger.

The Merger

James D. Oliver was the founder of the Oliver Chilled Plow Works. He was born in Scotland on August 28, 1823, and came to the United States when he was 11 years old. He worked many different jobs, including a blacksmith's helper. In 1855, he bought interest in his first foundry where he manufactured Sulky Plows. The Sulky Plow was a riding plow with one or two bottoms that was normally pulled by three or four horses. At that time, cast iron was the material of choice for plows because it was inexpensive. But cast iron did not accept a polish, and dirt would not move easily over the plow blade surface. Sometimes, the plow could go only a few yards in gumbo soil and the operator would have to stop to clean the surface of the plow blade.

To solve this problem, Oliver developed a process of rapidly cooling, or "chilling," a chosen portion of the casting. This process created a very hard surface that could be polished and would allow dirt to pass over it easily. The result was a much better plow blade, commonly known as the chilled plow.

James D. Oliver died in 1908. His son, Joseph D. Oliver, who had worked in the company as a finan-

The third of the original Hart-Parr tractors saw 17 years of use on the farm before being donated to the Smithsonian Institution Museum of History and Technology in Washington, D.C. in 1949. *Floyd County Historical Society*

cial manager, became the chief executive officer after his father's death.

On April 1, 1929, the Hart-Parr Tractor Company of Charles City, Iowa, merged with Oliver Chilled Plow Works of South Bend, Indiana, and Nichols and Shepard Threshing Machine Company of Battle Creek, Michigan. The following month American Seeding Machine Company of Springfield, Ohio, joined the fold. Together these companies formed the Oliver Farm Equipment Company. The

This Hart-Parr No. 1 tractor, manufactured the winter and spring of 1902, was the first successful gasoline tractor. It was purchased by an Iowa farmer and used for several years. Neither this tractor nor the second Hart-Parr produced is still in existence. *Floyd County Historical Society*

The Hart-Parr Model 30-60 was built from 1911 to 1916. The tractor had hit-and-miss governing, one forward speed, and a 10x15-inch bore and stroke.

oldest of these companies, the Nichols and Shepard Threshing Machine Company was founded in 1848.

Joseph D. Oliver was elected chairman of the board of the new company. Melvin W. Ellis, president of Hart-Parr, became president of the new company and continued in that position until January 1, 1931, when C. R. Messinger became president and Ellis became a vice chairman of the board. The corporate headquarters were located at 400 W. Madison in Chicago.

As president of Chain Belt Company in Milwaukee, Wisconsin, C. R. Messinger had been intimately connected with the agricultural implement industry for 14 years, and his abilities as a manager gained recognition. He served on many boards of directors, including Milwaukee Gas Light Company, First Wisconsin National Bank, First Wisconsin Trust Company, First Wisconsin Company, Sivyer Steel Casting Company of Chicago and Milwaukee, Interstate Drop Forge Company, Federal Malleable Company, and Stearns Conveyor Company of Cleveland.

R. C. Rolfing was elected vice president and general manager of Oliver Farm Equipment soon after the merger in 1929. Under his leadership, the manufacturing plants were modernized to provide a generous supply of quality products for Oliver dealers. There have been many good comments about his contributions to the company.

W. A. Weed was elected vice president of Oliver Farm Equipment in late 1929. A. H. Witt continued as comptroller, a position that he held for many years with Hart-Parr before the merger. H. S. Lord was general sales manager and well regarded for his enthusiasm and knowledge of people and products.

Dave E. Darrah was advertising manager. His motto for 1930 was, "Tell 'em and sell 'em—these two jobs we can do this year!" In 1931, Darrah became ill and left Oliver. Bert C. King took over as ad manager and designed the Oliver shield and flag. Through the two men's efforts, modern literature on all of the products were made available to the dealers. A mailing was made to all farmers who owned Oliver products. The goal was to make them all-Oliver farm-

This 1913 Hart-Parr Model 30-60 was purchased by the Oliver Management Club in 1964 and was displayed in a Plexiglas enclosure in front of the Floyd County Courthouse for many years. When the Floyd County Historical Society developed the current museum in Charles City, the tractor was transferred to the society's custody.

ers. This all-Oliver prospects list was segmented by eight classifications: Canadian Wheat, Northwest Wheat, Southwest Wheat, Western Diversified, Eastern Diversified, Potatoes and Truck, Orchard and Southwest, and Cotton and South.

John L. Carpenter was treasurer. He had a good understanding of credits and collectibles. His training of branch employees and dealers about the financial aspects of the farm equipment business was excellent and helped the company succeed financially.

This merger was quite successful because the new company provided a full line of agricultural equipment, and Oliver Farm Equipment Company became a leader in the agricultural equipment industry.

The spirit of inventive enterprise that marked the early activities of the Hart-Parr Tractor Company continued with Oliver to produce many new developments to make the farmer's work easier, more efficient, and more profitable. Oliver was a leader in the development of products that would benefit society through cost effectiveness, interchangeability, safety, and other benefits to the owners.

Oliver Tractors for Russia

During the early 1930s, Russia sought to purchase tractors and combines from the United States. The Russian representatives came a few days earlier than expected, and Oliver was not ready to show the tractor designed to meet their specifications. To buy some time, Oliver officials contacted the Milwaukee and St. Paul Railroad while the Russians were en route and persuaded the railroad not to stop in Charles City but to continue to Mason City about 31 miles west. Some Oliver factory representatives met the train in Mason City, took the Russians to an elaborate breakfast, toured some farms in the Mason City area, and then after lunch traveled to Charles City. Meanwhile, others worked all night on the tractor so that it was ready to show to the Russians.

The Russians ordered 5,000 Oliver Model 28-44 tractors and 2,000 Model F combines. Oliver's shipment of the tractors and combines started in 1930 and was completed by 1931. The sale of the tractors from the Charles City plant and combines from Oliver's Battle Creek plant helped the company finan-

The Hart-Parr 30-60, the Old Reliable, in its heyday. Hart-Parr offered a wide selection of wheels for angle, spade, and spike lugs. In fact, the 12-24 and 18-36 models were offered with solid rubber treads on the front and rear wheels. Rubber treads were offered for use where conventional steel wheels and lugs were not permitted or were not practical. *Floyd County Historical Society*

The Hart-Parr 20-40 featured two forward speeds and was built from 1911 to 1914. This one was sold at auction in the summer of 1996. Thanks to a successful "Bring the Tractors Home" fund-raising campaign, the Floyd County Historical Society was able to buy it.

OLIVER

HART-PARR AND OLIVER CONTRIBUTIONS TO SOCIETY

Hart-Parr Contributions
- Replacement of steam engine power for agriculture
- Successful internal combustion tractor mass production
- First tractor production plant
- Kerosene-burning engine
- Oil-cooled engine
- Valve-in-head engine
- Independent power take-off
- Force-fed lubrication in tractor engines
- Gave the word "tractor" to the industry
- First foreign tractor business

Oliver Contributions
- Tricycle Row Crop tractor
- Economical, practical diesel tractor
- Practical independent power take-off
- Mass production of six-cylinder tractors
- Tip Toe wheels
- Electrical control of hydraulics
- Equalizer brake pedals
- Double-disc brakes in tractors
- Low-pressure engine lubricating system
- Aluminized steel mufflers
- Tilt and telescoping steering wheel
- Four-wheel drive with Terra tires
- Wheel guard fuel tanks
- Certified horsepower
- Two-point hitch and lower link draft control
- Cast-iron grille for Row Crop front stability
- Ridemaster seat
- Electric lights
- Bale Thrower
- Throw-away Raydex Shares

The Little Red Devil, also called the Little Devil or Red Devil, was Hart-Parr's response to the growing demand for small tractors. The tractor had two speeds in forward or reverse.

Hart-Parr's Little Red Devil used a single rear drive wheel. Only 725 serial numbers were issued for this rare Hart-Parr model. This one was purchased by the Floyd County Historical Society in 1996 in the "Bring the Tractors Home" campaign.

cially early in the Great Depression. After the Russian tractor order was filled, the Oliver tractor plant was closed, except for a few people in the engineering department who were working on the Model 70 tractor design. Those remaining included Archie Howland, who was in charge of accounting; Jim Smith, who was in charge of shipping and repair orders; and Edna Ladd, who was secretary to the plant manager but was moved to the switchboard to take incoming calls that were primarily for repairs. One year she worked all summer without pay. She continued to work for Oliver for 45 or more years.

Further Corporate Changes

In 1944, Oliver bought the Cleveland Tractor Company of Cleveland, Ohio, and the name was changed from Oliver Farm Equipment to The Oliver Corporation. The acquisition of Cleveland, with its line of crawler tractors, expanded Oliver's focus from just farm equipment to industrial products as well.

From 1944 to 1960, Oliver acquired several more companies, including Be-Ge of Gilroy, California, a hydraulic equipment manufacturer; Farquhar-Iron Age of York, Pennsylvania, which made equip-

Although archival photographs of the Little Red Devil showed a cowling covering the engine, this restored model does not have one. In 1914, full coverage body work was a radical concept for tractors.

The Little Red Devil used a two-cylinder two-cycle engine with a 5 1/2x7-inch bore and stroke. The two-cycle engine could run in either direction. Oddly enough, the tractor was put in reverse by switching the engine's direction.

ment for potatoes and conveyors; and Chris Craft Outboard Motors. Some of these acquisitions were not profitable and did not help the company.

I recall a disheartening situation when I was privileged to review some confidential financial information. During the first quarter of 1958, the tractor plant at Charles City had accounted for several million dollars net profit. The Battle Creek harvesting plant was in its off-season but still accounted for about $160,000 net profit. The Cleveland crawler tractor plant was breaking even. The other seven plants showed losses amounting to about three-fourths of the profit from the Charles City tractor plant and the Battle Creek harvesting plant.

In 1960, White Motor Corporation bought some of Oliver's plants, including the plant that manufactured tillage equipment in South Bend, Indiana; the hay equipment plant in Shelbyville, Illinois; the tractor plant in Charles City; the harvesting equipment plant in Battle Creek; and the seeding equipment plant in Springfield, Ohio. The name changed again, from The Oliver Corporation to

The Oliver flag on this 1930 Row Crop advertisement shows the four components of the 1929 merger that made the Oliver Farm Equipment Company: Hart-Parr, Nichols and Shepard, Oliver, and American Seeding Companies. *Floyd County Historical Society*

UPPER LEFT: Oliver maintained a tie to its Hart-Parr roots with tractors such as this 18-27 Row Crop labeled Oliver Hart-Parr. The Oliver Hart-Parr 18-27 Row Crop was built from 1930 to 1937 and was available with one or two front wheels. This 18-27 Row Crop is outfitted with an Oliver planter.

Oliver Corporation, a subsidiary of White Motor Corporation. The remaining plants became a part of Amerada Hess. Finally, in the early 1960s, White bought the Cleveland line of crawlers and the contents of the plant, which they moved to Charles City, and this, too, became a part of Oliver Corporation.

In 1961, White Motor Company purchased Cockshutt of Canada and made it a part of Oliver Corporation. The next year, White Motor Company bought Minneapolis-Moline but operated it as a subsidiary of White Motor Company separate from Oliver Corporation because of U.S. antitrust laws.

From approximately 1960 to 1966, Oliver was a major source of profit for White Motor Company. The farm equipment business went into a minor recession in the late 1960s and White Motor executives criticized Oliver, Minneapolis-Moline, and Cockshutt for not contributing enough to the overall company profit. But the farm equipment profit, as a percentage of sales, was greater than that of the truck division.

In late 1969, Oliver, Cockshutt, and Minneapolis-Moline were merged into one organization called the White Farm Equipment Company, Division of White Motor Corporation. The division's headquarters were established in Hopkins, Minnesota. Over the next five years, the individual company names disappeared and all of the colors were changed to the two-tone gray color of the White models. After 1975, the names Oliver, Minneapolis-Moline, and Cockshutt no longer appeared on the tractors manufactured at Charles City, Iowa.

White Motor Company had economic problems during the late 1970s. In December 1980, Texas Investment Corporation purchased White Farm Equipment Company, Division of White Motor Company, and operated it as a wholly owned subsidiary. In November 1985, selected assets of White Farm Equipment Company were purchased by Allied Products Corporation. In 1986, White Farm Equipment purchased selected assets from White Farm Manufacturing Ltd. in Canada. In May 1987, White Farm Equipment merged with another Allied subsidiary to form White-New Idea Farm Equipment Company with headquarters in Coldwater, Ohio.

The cover of the 1936 Oliver catalogue shows the advantages of the Oliver Row Crop tractors, including the Tip Toe wheels, which gave the rear wheels adequate traction without compacting the topsoil. *Floyd County Historical Society*

OPPOSITE: Oliver's first Row Crop tractors were designed in 1928. Row Crop models used a tricycle or narrow-front design. The maneuverability, ground clearance, and ability to straddle rows made Row Crop tractors ideally suited to cultivation. *Floyd County Historical Society*

The Oliver Hart-Parr 18-27, which was available with a single front wheel in 1930 and 1931 and with a dual front wheel from 1930 to 1937.

The next change in ownership was in June 1991 when AGCO purchased the Charles City plant. The next year, after 86 years of tractor manu-facturing in Charles City, Iowa, the plant was closed. On October 29, 1993, there was an auction to sell what was left of the Charles City tractor plant. The plant was demolished during the fall of 1995. The powerplant smokestack was imploded December 8, 1995, and the rest of the powerplant was torn down by January 1, 1996.

Although the company no longer exists, the Oliver brand is kept alive by a large number of dedi-cated Oliver customers and the Hart-Parr/Oliver Collectors Association. The association had more than 3,000 members in 1996, and membership is growing. Some of the collectors have as many as 100 historical and restored tractors.

POWER ON TIPTOE

18 DRAWBAR

CENTRAL TOOL MOUNTING

STEERING – BRAKING

TIPTOE WHEELS

OLIVER ROW CROP

OLIVER FARM EQUIPMENT SALES COMPANY

DEVELOPMENT OF THE FLEETLINE TRACTORS

In 1940, Oliver began research to develop all of the applications, configurations, accessories, and special tractors that would become part of a new tractor line—the Oliver Fleetline. These tractors were to be new from the ground up.

The Oliver 60, 70, and 80 models had been quite successful, but they were designed individually without much consideration of other models, interchangeability of parts, or component assemblies. Another consideration was to quiet the tractors down to the range of 85 decibels or lower at the operator's ear. Improved overall appearance and styling, engine options for different fuels, practical independent power take-off, maximum interchangeability of parts among the three models , and the well-being of the operator were among the most important items guiding the design of the Oliver Fleetline.

Row Crop Tractors

Oliver registered two patents for the row-crop badge with a rectangular bar and for the Oliver/Hart-Parr row-crop logo on December 30, 1929. In those patents, the company claimed to have been using this logo since November 8, 1929.

Row Crop tractors had larger diameter rear tires than the Standard tractors. This provided adequate clearance for most crops. Some crops, such as sugar cane, require more crop clearance depending upon the method of growing the crop.

HERE'S
PROOF
OF A NEW WORLD OF
POWER

WHAT THE TEST ENGINEERS HAVE DISCOVERED—
AND WHAT FARMERS HAVE PROVED IN THE FIELD

CONFIDENTIAL

KEEP 'EM PLOWING

. . . A REPORT ON THE
ROW CROP 60 NEBRASKA TRACTOR TEST
(AND WHAT THIS TEST MEANS)

The tricycle Row Crop tractors came in two versions. The dual front wheel was the most popular in the 1940s and 1950s. It had two small front tires and wheels mounted close together so that they could pass between two rows when cultivating crops such as corn. The single front wheel was similar to the dual front-wheel version, except that it had one larger wheel in front instead of the smaller two wheels. The single front-wheel version was used primarily for cultivating special vegetable crops such as asparagus.

In the mid-1950s, after Ferguson and Massey-Harris merged to form Massey-Ferguson, the company sent a letter threatening Oliver with a lawsuit for patent infringement on single front-wheel tractors. Massey-Ferguson had just received a patent on its model, but Oliver had advertised and sold single front-wheel tractors since the 18-27 Row Crop in 1930. Copies of advertising literature and a dated assembly drawing were sent to the Massey-Ferguson Legal Department proving that the patent was worthless.

Another popular Row Crop version in the 1940s had an adjustable front axle. It became popular because it was more stable than the tricycle types. The front axle width was adjustable for various row spacings and high enough to have about the same crop clearance as the rear-axle housings. This also allowed the front tires to be aligned with the rear tires so the rear tires would make tracks within the tracks made by the front tires.

The Oliver Fleetline tractors represented a shift in Oliver's approach to new models. Designed with part and component group interchange in mind, the new line was engineered for maximum cost effectiveness. The new line also introduced a host of new features and an unprecedented emphasis on operator comfort.

ABOVE: This 1941 advertisement touts the Oliver 60 Row Crop, which produced 15.17 drawbar and 18.35 belt horsepower when tested at Nebraska in 1941 . *Floyd County Historical Society*

This 1942 Oliver Model 60 Standard tractor on steel wheels. The equalizer brake pedal system was used first on the Model 60 tractor and was patented by Oliver in the early 1940s. It could not be used by other companies without a license or permission from Oliver.

This Oliver industrial tractor equipped with dual rear wheels is preparing a roadbed. It is most likely based on the Model 50, a four-cylinder tractor built from 1937 to 1948 that was available only in the standard tread configuration. *J.C. Allen & Son*

The extra-high-clearance Row Crop tractor had an adjustable front axle designed primarily for sugar cane fields in Louisiana, where the sugar cane is planted on ridges and the tires run in furrows. The design required approximately 12 inches more crop clearance than the regular Row Crop tractors. Drop gear housings with chain or gears as a drive mechanism were normally used to obtain the extra height. The front axle was adjustable, similar to the regular Row Crop, except that it had to be about 12 inches higher. This tractor looked as if it were on stilts. The rear wheels had deep lugs and the tires a large outside diameter that made the tractor suitable for operation in the muddy furrows. Another application was for cultivating special vegetable crops such as asparagus. Because of its specialized use, sales of this version were low compared to the other Row Crop versions.

Late in the 1940s, Oliver tractors were offered with either steel wheels or rubber tires. This 1942 Model 60 Standard has rubber tires.

Standard Tractor Configurations

Early Hart-Parr and other tractors were designed primarily for drawbar work—pulling plows, disk harrows, and other such implements. Some tractors also had a belt pulley mechanism to power stationary pieces of equipment, such as corn shellers, threshers, or rock crushers. These tractors were large and heavy with steel wheels and lugs that made them effective at pulling large implements in the field, but they were extremely slow.

Can you imagine a large tractor pulling plows with several 12-inch bottoms at about 1 1/2 miles per hour? Some stories that have come from the large wheat fields of Montana tell of farmers who plowed until noon to reach the end of the field, ate their lunch, then plowed till dark to get back home. I've heard of a farmer who had a cabin at one end of his field where he slept at night, and then spent the next day plowing to get back home.

The many different tractor configurations needed to meet customer requirements were considered during the early stages of planning the new Oliver Fleetline tractors. The term "Standard" was introduced by Oliver to distinguish the common tractor configuration used for drawbar and belt drive from the new Row Crop tractors. The Standard tractors had a fixed-tread front axle and fixed or limited rear-axle tread adjustment. The front axle was low and did not provide for much crop clearance. It was about the same height as the center of the front wheel. The rear tires had a smaller outside diameter than the Row Crop tractors. The Wheatland version was the Standard tractor used where there were large fields of small grain and little or no requirement to cultivate row crops.

The Orchard version was similar to the Standard except it had a larger sheet metal cowling to slide under tree limbs and to protect the operator. The steering wheel and operator's seat were lower and farther back, and the steering wheel was placed below the special cowling so that it would not interfere with tree limbs.

Some customers thought they knew a better way to design a tractor. During the late 1940s a customer named Hutchinson from Orlando, Florida, was not satisfied with Oliver's orchard tractor. He

The Row Crop 60 was powered by an Oliver four-cylinder engine with a 3 5/16x3 1/2-inch bore and stroke. The tractor weighed in at 2,450 pounds with rubber tires on 9-32 rear and 5-15 front wheels.

commented that Oliver did not know how to design a good orchard tractor. Chief engineer Louis Gilmer invited him to Charles City to tell the engineering department how to design a better one.

He insisted that the operator's seat be able to pivot to different operator positions and that it be easily removed from its mounting without the use of tools for those times when the seat was not needed because of equipment attached to the tractor. Parts were made and installed according to Hutchinson's instructions.

Next came the trial to check out the tractor with the newly made parts. It was tested on E Street, which ran through the plant area. South of the plant were three sets of railroad tracks. Hutchinson drove the tractor south on E Street across the railroad tracks, turned the tractor around, opened the throttle wide in sixth gear, and drove back across the tracks at about 17 miles per hour. The seat came loose from its support and left Hutchinson and the seat on the railroad tracks. The tractor crashed into cars parked between the plant's buildings on E Street. The first car was totaled, the second car had considerable damage, and the third and

fourth cars required some repair. Hutchinson's parting comments were, "I am sorry about the accident. I hope that you understand what I was trying to accomplish. I leave the tractor design to you."

The Ricefield version was similar to the Standard. The main difference was that the rear tires had deeper lugs to allow the wheels to penetrate through the water and mud in a rice field to the more solid surface underneath. Moving parts that would normally be below the top of the water in the rice field were sealed.

The Industrial version was similar to the Standard except that the front axle was strengthened to support heavy front-end loads when implements such as front-end loaders were attached. The rear-axle carrier was also strengthened to support rear-end loads for attachments such as a backhoe. It came with front and rear tires that had higher load-carrying capacities to support the heavier loads. Low bar tread tires were used when operating on paving or compacted soil. Diamond-tread tires were used in sand and sandy soil conditions.

Styling

By the mid-1930s, Oliver began to design tractors for looks as well as for function. The belief was that the farmers' wives were influencing the purchases of farm equipment with visual appeal being one factor in the decision.

In 1935, the improved styling on the Model 70 included an enclosed engine compartment. In 1938, the Oliver 70 appearance was improved again. In 1940, the Oliver 60 was introduced with new styling to match the 1938 restyled Oliver 70.

The design of the new styling for the Oliver Fleetline tractors was started in 1942. In 1944, six experimental prototypes of each of the Model 66, 77, and 88 were built for test and development purposes. These tractors were known as XL, XM, and XK, respectively. Because the styling of these experimental tractors resembled the Model 60, it was not obvious that these tractors were of a new design when they were observed in the field while being tested. Also, Oliver engineering needed more time to complete the new design for an effective introduction to the public.

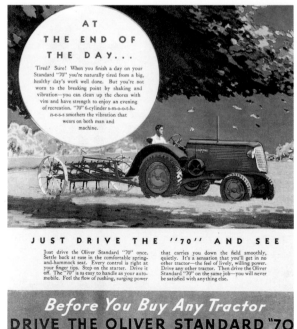

In the 1940s Oliver introduced a Row Crop tractor with a front axle that could be adjusted to fit the distance between crop rows. This 1946 Model 60 Row Crop has an adjustable front axle.

This 1938 advertisement shows the standard tractor configuration, which also received the new styling treatment. *Floyd County Historical Society*

31

A 1935 Oliver Hart-Parr Row Crop 70, the first year for the new model. The 70 featured an Oliver six-cylinder engine rated at 1,500 rpm that could be equipped to burn gasoline or distillate. The distillate model weighed in at 3,900 pounds. The first mass-produced agricultural tractor to offer electric lights as an option was the Oliver 70 Row Crop in 1937.

To assist with the new look, Oliver employed industrial design consultant Wilbur Henry Adams to work with all of the Oliver plants. One of my first assignments in October 1944 was to work with him to design the wheel guards for the new Fleetline tractors. Wilbur would make an artist's sketch of a plan compatible with the overall design of the tractor. It was then my job to make a design layout and complete the details of his sketch to fit the tractors.

Wilbur was primarily concerned with eye appeal; he had no responsibility for the tooling and product cost. When a design was complete, it was my responsibility to review it with our manufacturing engineering department to obtain preliminary cost estimates. Wilbur's designs were beautiful and exotic for that era. I learned much from him, but his first designs cost far more than we could afford. So I received permission to propose my own design, which was influenced more by cost estimates and suggestions from our manufacturing engineering department.

My design could be made in two sizes, and by having some extra holes tapped in the flange of the axle carrier, the wheel guards could be interchange-

able for both the left and the right sides of the tractor. The larger wheel guard fit the tractors with the larger tires of the Row Crop type, while the smaller wheel guard fit the tractors with smaller tires, such as the Wheatland. Wilbur agreed with the need for some compromises in his designs.

Most tractor wheel guards had lamp brackets bolted to the wheel guard's sheet metal. Within a few years, the metal often cracked around the lamp bracket. I was determined that such a problem would not exist on my design. Three formed channels were designed to make the wheel guard strong and provide a secure means of attaching it to the axle carrier. To avoid failure of the metal around the lamp bracket, the attaching bolts were to go through the lamp bracket, through the wheel guard, and through the channel. I am not aware of any failure of the wheel guard around the lamp bracket on any of the Fleetline tractors. My wheel guard design lasted until the Oliver 1800 and 1900 tractors were introduced in 1960. Many of the competitive tractors in the United States and foreign countries copied the important points of this design.

I also designed extensions for the two sizes of wheel guards. These extensions were released as kits that could be added to the tractors before or after they were sold.

I was also involved with the sheet metal styling design in other areas that were my responsibility for the final design, including the transmission, differential, final drive, mechanical power lift, pulley, power take-off, seat, and related parts for all three Fleetline 66, 77, and 88 tractors. I was often referred to as the "rear-end man." My job was to follow the different styling changes through to the final design.

During late 1945 and early 1946, a pilot run of 300 Model 88 (XK) tractors were manufactured to test the market. The sheet metal was similar to that of the Model 60, so the new styling could be kept a secret until the introduction of the complete Fleetline. Meanwhile, we used interchangeable parts and low-cost tooling until the final design was agreed upon by Oliver management, sales, engineering, manufacturing engineering, and all others concerned. The pilot lot of Model 88 tractors was quickly accepted.

Finally, during 1946 the new styling was approved, and 300 Model 77s and 66s were manufactured to test the market.

Engines

One of the critical elements of Oliver's famous Fleetline tractors was the design of the engines. Determining the sizes of the engines was critical to the success of the full line of tractors. The final decision was to design a four-cylinder engine that would provide a net belt pulley or power take-off of 22 horsepower for the Model 66. The Model 77 engine was to be a six-cylinder of the same bore and stroke, giving a net horsepower of 33. The Model 88 engine was to be a larger six-cylinder that would provide a net horsepower of 44 from the belt pulley or the power take-off.

Another challenge was determining where to build the engines. There were not enough laborers

Both the gasoline and distillate version of the 1936 Oliver Hart-Parr Row Crop 70 were tested at Nebraska. The gasoline tractor was rated for 26.57 horsepower, while the distillate version was rated slightly lower, at 24.8.

available in the Charles City area to build 25,000 to 30,000 tractors per year and also manufacture the engines. Waukesha Motor Company in Waukesha, Wisconsin, had manufactured the Oliver 60 and 80 engines and was quite interested in a contract with Oliver to build the engines for the new Fleetline tractors. Charles City plant representatives worked with Waukesha's president, James Delong, vice president of sales, Frederick Schulze, and senior project engineer, Roger Merriam. Merriam was assigned to work full time on the Oliver account. We had a great working relationship with these gentlemen, so our agreement was long-lived.

We worked out an arrangement with McCoy Truck Lines using two trucks, one operating in Iowa and the other in Wisconsin. The Iowa truck transported the engine castings from Oliver's foundry in

Three different styles of "Oliver Row Crop" decals were used from 1935 to 1938. The last decal change took place in October 1937, when the Model 70 was upgraded. This is another look at the 1936 Oliver Hart-Parr Row Crop 70.

The body work of the 70 was streamlined in October of 1937 for the 1938 production models. The look was one that caught on. By the mid-1940s, most of the tractors on the market were streamlined or styled in some fashion. This is a 1937 Oliver Row Crop 70 wide-front.

Charles City to Prairie du Chien where they were picked up by the Wisconsin truck and taken to Waukesha Motors plant in Waukesha. On the return trip the Wisconsin truck took a trailer load of engines to Prairie du Chien where they were picked up by the Iowa truck and taken to the Charles City plant assembly line. Interstate Commerce Commission regulations and economic considerations made this arrangement advantageous.

To obtain maximum power and fuel economy from the steadily increasing octane rating—expected to be 74 when the tractors would begin production—Oliver selected a compression ratio of 6.75:1 for the gasoline engine. For the engine that burned kerosene—a fuel with a 35 octane rating—a compression ratio of 4.75:1 was selected. A compression ratio of 15:1 was selected for the engine that would burn diesel—a fuel with a 40 cetane rating. The rated and governed speed of these engines was 1,600 rpm. The Oliver diesels quickly became so successful that the kerosene engines lost their appeal.

Tests at Waukesha Motor Company determined that the peak combustion pressure for the diesel engine was approximately 1,100 psi. The peak combustion pressure for the gasoline engine was approximately 850 psi. Oliver chose to apply many of the diesel engine principles to its gasoline engine to achieve high brake mean effective pressure. The crankcase and all other parts below the cylinder head were common across all engines. This design strategy produced both rugged and precision spark-ignition engines with excellent fuel economy and durability.

The most popular Row Crop tractor in the early 1940s had dual front wheels. This 1939 Model 70 tractor shows an improved appearance compared to the previous models.

The orchard configuration tractor was a standard tread model with extra sheet metal over the wheels to prevent the tree limbs from catching on the tires. This is a 1946 Orchard 70 tractor.

Development of the Diesel Engine

The first 50 Model 88 diesel tractors were manufactured with the Ricardo combustion system in the cylinder head. There was not enough clearance on the Row Crop tractors to use a Robert Bosch or American Bosch inline multiple-plunger fuel injection pump. Neither of the Bosch manufacturers were interested in designing a single-plunger fuel-injection pump, so the first 50 Model 88 diesel tractors were assembled with an experimental single-plunger fuel injection pump manufactured by Sundstrand. The design of this single-plunger pump was a cooperative effort between Sundstrand, Waukesha, and Oliver. After these tractors were distributed in 1948, American Bosch proposed and then produced a single-plunger pump in time for the first production run of Model 88 diesels.

Later, the simpler and less costly Roosa fuel pump replaced the single-plunger Bosch fuel-injection pump. The initial dynamometer tests completed by Oliver's experimental engineering department were encouraging. Oliver continued to test the Roosa pump for several months and make recommendations for improvements. The pump was also installed on some of the test tractors in the field. The Roosa fuel-injection pump later became Oliver's choice for production.

Meanwhile, I was responsible for the final design of the transmission, differential, final drive, and other attachments and accessories behind the front frame of the tractor. Tests were conducted on Model 88 diesels and some experimental Model 66s and 77s near Bakersfield, California. I reviewed the weekly performance reports on each tractor and noted that at or below 40 degrees F the diesels were hard to start.

My brother Ray Morrell, who lived near Blue Mound, Kansas, wanted to buy a Model 88 gasoline tractor, so arrangements were made between our plant and the Kansas City sales branch. Then I got a call from the Kansas City branch saying that all of the gasoline Model 88s had been allocated, so they wanted to substitute a pilot run Model 88 diesel. I rejected the substitution because my brother had herds of livestock and needed a tractor that was reliable in cold weather. He got his gasoline Model 88 from the next production run.

Word of the rejection traveled quickly from the Kansas City branch to Oliver's Chicago office and then to Charles City. "Who is this engineer who doesn't want his brother to have a Model 88 diesel?" they asked. I explained why, and after that, the cylinder-head fuel-combustion system was changed to the Lanova system with the American Bosch single-plunger fuel-injection pump and the electric air intake heater, which provided a good cold weather starting diesel. In fact, some farmers said the Oliver diesel tractors started so well in cold weather that they used them to pull their gasoline automobiles to get them started.

Diesel Difficulties

Despite the ultimate success of the Oliver diesel, there were some developmental difficulties. Because of the short development time of the American Bosch single-plunger pump, the control linkage did not last long. When the linkage failed, the fuel meter fell down and let the engine run above the rated rpm because of all of the extra fuel. Fortunately, engine speed was limited by the size of the air-intake manifold.

As soon as the problem was discovered, the Charles City engineering department was in touch with American Bosch to build a better linkage. At Charles City, we designed a test that was severe enough to fail a production control within a few hours. Between our rigorous tests and the cooperative effort with American Bosch, a satisfactory control was constructed. We replaced the linkage in the tractors that had already been manufactured. I am not aware of any failures of the new control linkage.

Only a few control linkages failed in the field, but we heard some interesting reactions to these high-revving motors. One farmer thought the sound of the racing engine was an airplane about to crash near him, so he jumped off the tractor and hid by the rear wheel. He finally turned off the fuel supply to stop the engine. He then contacted his dealer for some service. The control was replaced and the farmer was back in operation again.

The operator's seat on orchard tractors was lowered and moved rearward for protection from tree limbs, and the steering wheel was protected by a special cowling.

A 1937 advertisement for the orchard configuration of the Model 70 tractor, which is badged as the Grove 70 here. Oliver used both the Orchard and Grove labels on their orchard models. *Floyd County Historical Society*

THE PEOPLE WHO DEVELOPED THE FLEETLINE TRACTORS

Oliver's Chicago Office

Many people contributed to the development of the famous Fleetline tractors during the 1940s and early 1950s, including those in Oliver's executive office in Chicago. Alva Phelps became chairman of the board of directors soon after joining Oliver in 1944. He was formerly employed by the Saginaw Steering Gear Division of General Motors. The highly efficient recirculating ball steering mechanism was his invention. The principle of his invention was to use the lower resistance of steel balls rolling in grooves rather than use conventional gear steering to control a vehicle. The friction between gear teeth and a worm gear in a conventional steering mechanism was far less efficient and less responsive than the recirculating ball. Because of his engineering skills, Phelps was a strong booster of the Fleetline tractor development program.

A. King McCord was president of Oliver during the late 1940s until late 1954 or early 1955, when he became president of Westinghouse Airbrake Company. Of all the chief executives, I enjoyed him most in meetings about products, engineering, future planning, and many other aspects of our company. He was down to earth, a good listener, and always appeared unselfish. His efforts were for the good of the company.

In 1942, Oscar Eggen became Oliver's vice president of engineering. He had been chief engineer of the tractor plant in Charles City when the Oliver Farm Equipment Company was formed. He had ample experience and good knowledge of farm equipment, particularly about tractors. He was full of good suggestions and was skilled at planning and defining product requirements. He resigned in 1954 to become a manufacturer's representative in the Los Angeles area.

Roy Melvin was vice president of manufacturing. He had once been plant manager at Charles City. His expertise was in industrial engineering, but he had some health problems and resigned his position in the executive office. After recuperating, he returned to the Charles City plant as supervisor of the methods department, which was also known as the industrial engineering department.

Joe and Merle Tucker were brothers in Oliver's executive office. Merle was vice president of sales. Joe resigned shortly after I started with Oliver. He had an idea for a self-propelled combine, but he could not get his idea accepted at the combine plant in Battle Creek or in Oliver's executive offices. So Joe took his idea to the Massey-Harris Company in Racine, Wisconsin. They listened to his idea, and the Massey-Harris combine was so successful that it became a standard for a long-lived harvesting system. Massey-Harris merged with Ferguson of England in the late 1950s and became Massey-Ferguson Company. Joe's next move was to the New Holland Company of New Holland, Pennsylvania.

Black and White were two young fellows who traveled together to maintain contact with sales offices. Black left Oliver after a short stint, but White was Samuel Walter White Jr., son of Samuel W. White Sr., a member of the board of directors. Sam Sr. was the Chicago investment banker who helped form the new Oliver Farm Equipment Company from four family-owned businesses in 1929.

Sam White Jr. started as a trainee in 1939 at South Bend. He spent 1942–1946 in the U.S. Navy. After the war, he held several positions in the corporation, including president of Oliver International S. A., the company's export subsidiary. In 1960, he became president of the new Oliver Corporation, a subsidiary of White (no relation) Motor Corporation. During the last part of his Oliver association, he was White Motor's executive vice president of farm and industrial equipment. Sam Jr. was highly knowledgeable about agriculture and industry. He worked tirelessly to gain recognition for Oliver products and their capabilities.

J. Oliver Cunningham, a grandson of founder Joe Oliver, was in Oliver's advertising department during the latter stages of the Fleetline tractor development. Later, he became the manager of the Memphis, Tennessee, sales branch. J. Oliver and I had fun playing and winning at bridge during evenings when he came to Charles City to develop advertising programs. He resigned from the company and moved to Arizona, where he sold appliances and developed his hobbies.

These are only some—there are many others who also deserve recognition—of the Oliver executives involved directly with the development of the famous Fleetline 66, 77, and 88 tractors.

Charles City Plant Operating Committee

George W. Bird, Oliver's Charles City plant manager, operated an Old Reliable in Montana when he was a youth around 1915. He looked at the tractor nameplate and noted that it was built by Hart-Parr in Charles City. He decided that he would rather build tractors than drive them. He came to Charles City and began a very interesting life with Hart-Parr and Oliver.

The Charles City plant had an operating committee made up of the chief supervisors and some assistants who met each Wednesday at noon. The food was catered by the St. Charles Hotel or a local restaurant. After lunch, members reported on the various phases of plant operation.

In addition to the operating committee members shown in the photo in this section, several others also participated on the operating committee during the design and manufacture of the Oliver Fleetline tractors. Gordon Atherton became foundry superintendent when E. A. Brunsman retired. Ernie Williamson became chief purchasing agent after Bill Kuehn's retirement. Frank Pryatel became plant manager in 1961 after George Bird's retirement. Dick Bennett took over as chief metallurgist when Phil Carbaugh retired. After Ed Kroft went to the White Farm Equipment office in Hopkins, Minnesota, John Culbertson became personnel manager and retained that position until the plant closed in late 1992.

This operating committee was one of the hardest working and dedicated groups in the industry. The cooperation among the various departments was outstanding during the time the Fleetline tractors were designed, developed, and produced. We used some efficiency and management techniques that have been reported in recent years as if they were new.

Oliver Chief Engineer Herb Morrell attending a 1954 SAE meeting at Chicago's Edgewater Beach Hotel with business associate and friend Kip Recor, a sales representative for Torrington, a company that supplied straight roller bearings to Oliver. Author collection

Oscar Eggen, vice president of Oliver Engineering, is driving a Model 66 Industrial tractor that is pulling a trailer load of sightseers during the 1952 Tired Business Men's Golf Tournament at Charles City. Carl Rabe

Oliver Engineering Personnel

The planning of the Fleetline tractors was initially the responsibility of Oscar Eggen, vice president of engineering; chief engineer Louis Gilmer; assistant chief engineer Milford Stewart; and Tom Martin, supervisor of experimental engineering. During the mid-1940s, Bob Butler was hired as service manager and John Dorwin as assistant service manager. The service department, which reported to the engineering department, was responsible for the technical publications, including the operator's manual, parts catalog, service manual, and service bulletins.

John Selim was hired in 1945 as the industrial tractor sales representative. He also worked with outside suppliers to provide loaders and other attachments for the industrial tractors. During the late 1940s, John was transferred to Cleveland to work with the industrial sales department.

Over the next 20 years there were a few changes in the Charles City plant engineering leadership. In 1946, Milford Stewart went to South Bend as chief engineer of the Oliver plant there. Tom Martin then became the assistant chief engineer of the Charles City plant while Pete Burns took his place as supervisor of experimental engineering. Homer Dommel became his assistant. In 1948, Tom Martin went to Ohio as chief engineer of the Springfield plant. Bob Butler took his place as assistant chief engineer. John Dorwin became service manager, replacing Bob Butler, and Bill Brown became his assistant.

In 1950, Bob Butler went to South Bend to manage a new program on stationary power units. I replaced him as assistant chief engineer. When Louis Gilmer died in 1951, I replaced him as chief engineer, Pete Burns became assistant chief engineer, and Homer Dommel became supervisor of experimental engineering. In 1954, Pete Burns left

the company to become a member of the product planning department of Ford's tractor and implement division, so Ron Ronayne became assistant chief engineer.

In 1965, I moved to the Chicago office to become coordinator of outside products those products manufactured by another company for Oliver to sell through its dealer organization. Ron Ronayne then became chief engineer of the Charles City plant, and Bob Prunty became his assistant.

Some of the principal design engineers during the development of the Fleetline tractors were Wendell Neland on sheet metal, Walt Roeming on engines, Charles Van Overbeke on engines, Don Kinch on transmissions, myself on power take-off and pulley and general accessories behind the front frame, and Joe Pieper on front frame and front end in general. Chuck Ruhl was assigned the design of the new Hydra-Lectric hydraulic system.

Roy Sobolik was in charge of the drafting department, which made and checked all drawings. Among the draftsmen was Harrison Lambkin, who checked designs and drawings. Harrison was an unusual but accomplished person. He contracted polio at age four and was handicapped. He educated himself through correspondence courses and excelled in mathematics. He was George Bird's brother-in-law.

The specifications department was responsible for filing the tractor drawings, providing part numbers, and compiling and typing the bills-of-material from which the tractors would be manufactured and assembled. Ray Hennagir was the supervisor of this department at the outset of the Fleetline program. He retired shortly after the experi-

George W. Bird is sitting on the front wheel of an Old Reliable tractor he operated as a youth in Valier, Montana. He came to Charles City and was hired by Hart-Parr. He had many positions, working up to plant manager in 1944, a position he held until 1961 when he retired. Floyd County Historical Society

The Charles City Plant Operating Committee was responsible for the development of the famous Fleetline 66, 77, and 88 tractors. The photo was taken December 21, 1951. Outside row, from left: E. A. Brunsman, foundry superintendent; Ralph Battey, production control; Herb Stoakes, service manager; Bill Kuehn, chief purchasing agent; Archie Howland, supervisor of accounting; Lyle Lenth, maintenance superintendent; Roy Melvin, methods superintendent; Herb Morrell, chief engineer; George Bird, plant manager; Melvin Finch, general factory superintendent; Lloyd Maby, production control supervisor; Merle Tucker, vice president of sales at Oliver's Chicago office; Jim Martin, methods department; George Taylor, accounting department; John Rockufeler, supervisor of part machining; and Bob Burgraff, suggestion secretary. Inside row, from left: Russell Elliott, production control and special assignment; Merle Hicks, sales order manager; Dale Tower, maintenance department; Phil Carbaugh (nearly hidden), chief metallurgist; Lloyd Boyle, shop superintendent; Ed Kroft, personnel manager; Tony Obermeier, supervisor of assembly line and later shop superintendent; Leland Hartwell, chief inspector; Pete Burns, assistant chief engineer. Carl Rabe

This shows the evaluation of a Timken bearing design in the early 1950s. Pictured, from left, are Herb Morrell, George Curtis, and his replacement, all of Timken Bearing, and George Bird, Oliver's Charles City plant manager. In the background is Ida Smalley, Oliver's engineering department secretary. Carl Rabe

mental models were manufactured. Morrie Thelen, his assistant, became the supervisor and continued until the plant closed.

As assistant methods superintendent under Roy Melvin, Art Munson worked on the special tooling and dies for forming sheet metal and machines. Bob Lockhart, also in the methods department, worked on jigs and fixtures to machine castings and other parts.

The experimental engineering department performed all of the testing of the tractors and assemblies, such as the transmission, pulley mechanism, power take-off, and hydraulics. Keith Minard, Gene Lockie, and Max Denham were excellent electrical dynamometer operators and were also good at setting up field tests. Each tractor model had to be tested at the University of Nebraska in order to sell that model in the state of Nebraska. Max Denham accompanied most of the tractor models to Nebraska and assisted with the tests. Charlie Adams was unusually gifted at visualizing a test for one part or an assembly of parts. He had experience at the University of Nebraska and was familiar with various types of testing equipment before coming to Oliver. Joe Roland had a good personality for managing a remote or local tractor field test program.

One of the most valuable employees in engineering was Ida Smalley, secretary to the chief engineer at the Charles City plant. She had a firm knowledge of what was happening in the department and kept me informed of her evaluations. On big mail days she scanned and categorized the mail into as many as five piles: junk mail, reports with some notations by her, information only, to be answered, and emergency action required. She was a fast typist and typed all of the letters going out of the engineering department.

When she retired in 1961, she had been secretary to the chief engineer of the Charles City tractor plant for at least 42 years. I knew that it would be difficult to replace her. I sent two young women to Ida to be trained. This was unsatisfactory, however, because she made such great demands that both of them refused to accept the position.

Mildred Block, who worked in the accounting department, was a good prospect. I decided to let Ida retire, and then Mildred and I would work together on her training. Mildred soon became an efficient secretary.

One could not ask for a more dedicated group of people to create a whole new line of tractors.

Suppliers

Oliver made every part that was economical and practical to make and purchased those parts or assemblies that were not. Suppliers of standard and special parts made important contributions to the development of the Fleetline 66, 77, and 88 tractors. Manufacturers of large production standard parts are specialists in their own businesses. A good example is the tapered roller, roller, and ball bearing makers. It would not be economical for a farm equipment manufacturer to make bearings, hardware, and many other standard parts for their own low-production requirements.

William (Bill) Kuehn, Oliver's chief purchasing agent, had a big job coordinating all of the purchased items. These included materials such as steel, coke for the foundry, pig iron, scrap iron, and thousands of standard items. There was a radio program in the 1940s and 1950s called *Mr. Keene: Tracer of Lost Persons*. Sometimes Bill jokingly was called, "Mr. Kuehn, Tracer of Lost Purchases." Bill was never happy about such remarks because he and his department did their best to manage inventory and have purchased items delivered on schedule. One of their inventory management goals was to have only a three-day supply of engines and no more than a five-day supply of tires on hand.

Sales and Service

Sales and service functions were extremely important. The entire country was divided into sales branches, each of which was divided again into several territories. Each year, new territory managers were sent to Charles City to learn all of the sales points of Oliver tractors. Each fall, branch sales managers went to school so they could train the territory managers. Branch and territory managers were Oliver employees, but some independent distributors were also included in the sales and service schools. Coop Federee from Montreal, Canada, was a good example. Special sales and service schools were held for this Quebec distributor.

Service schools were generally held during the third week in January. The branch service managers were sent to Charles City for a week's training on any new tractor and for a refresher course on the older units. The branch service managers were then to hold service schools for the dealer's mechanics in each territory manager's area.

If there was something new during the year, plant representatives were sent to the branches to conduct special sales and service schools. The Charles City plant had representatives assigned to the branches through the branch contact program. The purpose of this program was to provide Oliver with information from each branch about any problems and possible improvements. Each team consisted of about five representatives, including a captain from engineering and an alternate member.

My team covered branches in Harrisburg, Pennsylvania; Richmond, Virginia; Memphis, Tennessee; and Columbus, Ohio. Harrisburg was my branch. When the Hydra-Lectric unit was introduced, I spent one week in Harrisburg conducting a sales and service school for Harrisburg personnel in 1949. In 1950, I spent a week during early March on sales and service for Seabrook's personnel in New Jersey. This school was the result of Seabrook Farms purchasing 69 Oliver diesel tractors. Each contact representative spent three weeks at the branch, one week in the spring during the tillage and planting season, one week during the cultivating season, and one week during the harvesting season. The contact teams were effective from about 1948 to 1952, when the program ended. After that, engineering representatives were sent only as needed.

Most Oliver tractor sales were made by its agricultural and industrial dealer network. Special tractor sales were handled by the tractor plant sales representatives. Oliver tractors were shown at most state and county fairs, as well as at other local functions such as parades.

Selling the Oliver Diesel

We had one main problem to overcome at the beginning of our diesel program. Farmers were not eager to buy a diesel tractor because of the poor reputation of the International Harvester Company (IHC) Super M diesel, which had been unreliable. To provide farmers with an incentive to buy Oliver diesel tractors, we made the following offer: Buy an Oliver diesel and Oliver will send you a check for half of your first six months' fuel bill. This program sold a large number of diesels, and it cost Oliver only an average of $44 per tractor. Oliver owners began telling their neighbors about the fuel savings compared to the gasoline tractors. By 1954, before the competition caught up to Oliver, Oliver was selling 45 to 50 percent of all diesel agricultural tractors.

Engine Lubrication

Oliver patented a low-pressure spurt-type engine oil lubricating system, which forced lubricating oil through the crankshaft at a pressure of about 15 psi. A slot in the crankshaft registered with a slot in the connecting rod of each cylinder, which when registered, forced oil into the connecting rod. A limited amount of oil reached the cylinder wall from each connecting rod, and the oil consumption was decreased. This type of system was not practical, however, on tractors having full-load speeds above 1,600 rpm. The combination of speed and size of the slots caused concern at higher speeds.

The 1946 Orchard 70, from the left side. The Orchard 70 was built from 1936 to 1948.

1942 Oliver 80 with steel wheels. An Oliver Row Crop 80 tested at Nebraska in 1938 put out 27.13 drawbar and 36.33 belt horsepower. The tractor weighed in at 4,930 pounds.

OPPOSITE: 1942 Row Crop 80 on steel. The Row Crop 80 was built from 1937 to 1948.

One of the companies Oliver acquired, the Nichols and Shepard Threshing Machine Company was founded in 1848, so 1948 marked 100 years of manufacturing for Oliver. The introduction of the Fleetline 66, 77, and 88 became part of Oliver's Centennial Celebration. These new tractors were displayed at many state, county, and local fairs. Trade magazines used color pictures and listed their innovations in their advertising. Color brochures and posters, such as the "Three Beauties" shown here, were available to Oliver's dealers for distribution to potential customers.

Oliver Diesels at Seabrook Farms

Seabrook Farms of Seabrook, New Jersey, grew vegetables of nearly all types for Birds Eye, a company that sells frozen vegetables. Seabrook Farms started business during the Depression and was quite successful. Seabrook leased about 30,000 acres on its own and contracted with other farmers who grew vegetables on another 50,000 acres.

By 1949, Seabrook Farms was ready to replace its tractors. Some of the vegetables grown by the contract farmers were of higher quality than those grown by the company, and research revealed that all farmers were using the same fertilizer and general crop management techniques. The best vegetables, however, were grown by farmers who had Oliver tractors. They commented that the tractor and cultivator combination provided more accurate control. As one farmer explained it, "You can put the fertilizer and the cultivator shovels right where you want them." This survey, along with the Oliver diesel program, were major factors that led Seabrook Farms to begin replacing its tractors with Oliver diesels. In March 1950, Oliver held service

schools for Seabrook Farms employees to familiarize them with the 69 Oliver Diesel 66, 77, and 88 tractors it had purchased. This was the start of a program to replace approximately 300 tractors.

I was called back to Seabrook Farms in September 1950 to resolve a combination lubricating oil and fuel problem. They reported that one 88 diesel was using six quarts of oil per day and others had similar problems. Our specifications called for #2 diesel fuel in the summer and #1 diesel fuel in the winter for cold weather operation. We discovered that the lubricating oil supplied to Seabrook Farms by an Amoco dealer in Shiloh, New Jersey, was for gasoline engines and that the fuel was a mixture of kerosene and furnace oil. Furnace oil contained up to three times more sulfur than diesel fuel. Excessive sulfur in the fuel is bad news for diesel engines, particularly for those operating at or near full load, and the Seabrook tractors having the problems were operating at full load.

We examined the tractor that was reported to use six quarts of oil per day. The engine was so full of sludge that one could get no more than three-quarters of a quart of oil in it. The tractor operator had reported that he had to fill it with oil each day, and someone in the office had referred to the operator's manual and, noting that the oil capacity was six

The Oliver 66, 77, and 88 tractors were introduced at state fairs, local fairs, and at dealer's programs. This photo is typical of the setting for the introduction of the new line. Literature highlighting the new innovations featured on the tractors was also available.

quarts, had assumed the operator was adding that much each day.

We removed the oil pan and the valve cover. Both were so full of sludge that there were grooves in the sludge made by the moving parts of the engine. We carefully removed what sludge we could by hand, ordered a barrel of diesel flushing oil, changed the two large lubricating oil filters, and filled the crankcase with flushing oil. The tractor was operated at about half power for four hours. The valve cover and oil pan were then removed again to rid the engine of the remaining sludge. We repeated the four-hour cleaning operation one more time and then inspected the inside of the engine. It was clean and just like new.

The chief of the Amoco Research Center in Baltimore met with me and representatives of Seabrook Farms. We reviewed the problems and requested that Amoco immediately send a truck to each of the Seabrook Farms to deliver heavy-duty diesel lubricating oil, remove the lubricating oil for gasoline

engines, and replace the fuel mixture with #2 diesel fuel. Seabrook Farms and I assured Amoco that we would recommend another source for diesel products if they did not comply with our request. Amoco trucks were at Seabrook Farms the following Monday. There were no more fuel or lubricant problems at Seabrook Farms. But this story has a rather sad ending because 1951, 1952, and 1953 were extreme drought years in New Jersey. Seabrook Farms went into bankruptcy, and we did not replace anymore old tractors.

Independent Power Take-Off

There is a myth that Cockshutt of Canada was the first tractor with independent power take-off (PTO) in 1948. Actually, this is wrong for several reasons. First, the Hart-Parr 18-36 manufactured in 1928 had an independent PTO. Second, Oliver's pilot run of 300 88s with independent PTO was in customers' hands by early 1946. Oliver did not publish the independent PTO until 1948, when it introduced

The belt pulley was located on the right side of all three Fleetline tractors, the Model 66, 77, and 88. This shows the belt pulley on a 1950 Standard 66.

The Model 66 had a four-cylinder engine with 22 belt horsepower. This is a Row Crop 66.

the Fleetline 66, 77, and 88 with the new styling and other innovations. From the early 1930s to 1948, Oliver manufactured tractors for Cockshutt using the Oliver 60, 70, and 80 tractors with some special sheet metal, color, and decal treatment; but these were not offered with independent PTO.

Oliver's independent PTO established a trend, at least on larger tractors. A transmission-driven PTO was satisfactory for some implements, such as mowers. But other implements, such as pull combines, could easily become clogged. With the transmission-driven PTO, the tractor would have to be stopped, the transmission taken out of gear, and the clutch let out to clear the clog. This prompted manufacturers to install a separate engine on their implements, adding $1,000 to $2,000 to the cost of many implements in the early 1950s. Oliver introduced its independent PTO for a list price of about $125, allowing one tractor to be used with more than one implement. Implement manufacturers eventually stopped

adding separate engines to their implements, which saved farmers the cost of purchasing and maintaining these additional engines.

Development of the Independent PTO

My second main assignment at Oliver was to work with a project engineer, Don Kinch, to develop a rear-mounted combination belt pulley and PTO for the new Fleetline 66, 77, and 88 tractors. Power take-off means that power from the tractor engine is transmitted to an implement so that it can perform its function without a ground drive or some other means. My main contribution to this design was the control system, including the engaging lever and internal parts for engaging and disengaging the PTO clutch independent of the engine clutch.

The usual testing was set up in the experimental engineering department. One test continued at full load, which was equivalent to the engine power of the 88 tractor, while the clutch was engaged and disengaged frequently. If the unit operated under these extreme conditions for 100 hours or more without failure or problems, it would be considered satisfactory for a pilot lot production and further tests. This unit failed early in the test. The clutch failed, the unit overheated, and there were other problems. It was then April 1945 and a new design had to be accomplished quickly.

I was asked to give my evaluation during a meeting with chief engineer Louis Gilmer, assistant chief engineer Milford Stewart, and supervisor of experimental engineering Tom Martin. We agreed that there was not enough room at the rear of the tractor for a combination PTO and belt pulley. Besides, we predicted that the PTO would soon replace the belt pulley.

There were too many cost compromises in the combination belt pulley/PTO unit, so it was suggested that the belt pulley be a separate unit mounted in front of the transmission with the pulley on the right side of the tractor. I was asked to make a preliminary belt pulley design to determine if it would be feasible to locate the pulley in front of the transmission. Ultimately, such a design appeared to be satisfactory.

The independent PTO then took priority over the belt pulley. Don Kinch, an expert mathematician, was assigned to other parts for the Fleetline design. I was asked to be responsible for the design of the PTO and belt pulley units for the Fleetline 66, 77,

and 88 tractors. Design criteria were reviewed and timetables were established. September 1945 was the deadline for completing the design and testing of experimental models so that we would be ready for field tests. I was told that the design had to be good because we planned to release it for production and make casting patterns, fixtures, and tools for it during the field tests.

Previous PTOs had been driven from the tractor transmission so that the power to the PTO-

The Row Crop 77 was built from 1948 to 1954. The tractor was available with a six-cylinder gas or diesel engine. This 1949 model is distinguished by the yellow stripe on the top of the grille, a feature exclusive to 1948 and 1949 models.

This Row Crop 77 is powered by the Oliver six-cylinder gasoline-burning engine. The tractor is equipped with the mechanical power lift and independent PTO.

The Industrial Fleetline tractors were standard tread models with stronger axles and were available in both low-bar tread tires for work on paved surfaces and diamond-tread tires for work in sandy conditions. This is a 1952 Industrial 66.

A 1951 Orchard 66. An Oliver Standard 66 (running on gasoline) tested at Nebraska in 1949 delivered 16.96 drawbar and 22.31 belt horsepower. The tractor weighed in at 2,919 pounds.

driven implement stopped whenever the forward motion of the tractor stopped. This kind of PTO was not satisfactory under clogging conditions. This prompted manufacturers to install a separate engine on their implements, which added an additional $1,000 to $2,000 in the early 1950s. The ideal solution was an independent PTO driven by the tractor's engine which could be engaged and disengaged independently from the transmission. Oliver introduced its independent PTO for a list price of about $125 and one tractor could, of course, be used for more than one implement. The separate engines on implements were discontinued, so the introduction of the independent PTO became a great cost saving to Oliver's farmer customers.

The main design goal was to provide an independent PTO with its own clutch so that it could be engaged and disengaged regardless of the motion of the tractor. This was accomplished by using a tubular clutch shaft and transmission input shaft. The driveshaft to the PTO clutch was splined to the engine flywheel and passed through the clutch and transmission shafts to an independent clutch at the rear of the tractor.

This view of a 1951 Orchard 66 shows the streamlined cowling added to these models for ease of Operation among tree branches.

The pilot production plan was to manufacture 300 88s with the new independent PTO during late 1945 and early 1946. By May 1, I had the PTO design ready for the drafting department to make drawings of all the individual parts. Oliver's policy was that the designer would not make production drawings of his design or check them. This was to be done by someone else. Drafting was so busy with other parts of the tractors that they did not know when they could start on my design, so I made the production drawings of all of the parts. When I asked to get them checked, no design checker was available, so I checked the drawings myself and our specifications department released the drawings for experimental parts. We ordered three sets of parts—one for laboratory tests, one to be installed on an experimental 88 tractor for field tests, and the third set for repairs or a second field test unit.

Testing on the experimental PTO was completed with only minor changes. The field test was done

An Oliver 66 Diesel tested at Nebraska in 1951 produced 22.45 belt and 17.7 drawbar horsepower, which was comparable to the gasoline-burning model. This is a 1952 Industrial 66.

A Row Crop 77 Diesel was tested at Nebraska in 1950, producing 25.14 drawbar and 35.79 belt horsepower from the 194-cubic-inch Oliver diesel. This is a 1950 example.

OPPOSITE: When tested at Nebraska in 1949, the Row Crop 77 put out 25.75 drawbar and 34.34 belt horsepower. This is a 1950 model.

through a farmer who had a large acreage of crops and was a good customer of Thill Brothers Implement in Rose Creek, Minnesota. This farmer used the experimental Model 88 with a pull silage harvester to fill silos with cornstalks. Joe Roland was the field test engineer for the PTO field tests. These tests were also used to prove the experimental Model 88 tractor in general. Since there were good results from the tests in the laboratory and in the field, it was then full speed ahead to release the Model 88 tractor and PTO for the pilot run.

After the pilot run, we encountered some problems with the independent PTO. The long drive-shaft between the engine flywheel and the PTO clutch acted as a torsion spring to dampen shock loads. We chose Stressproof steel for the long drive-shaft because it was advertised to be strong and wear resistant, but advertising can be misleading. One of my first field trips for Oliver was in late spring 1946 to Herman Streakers Implement dealership in Wapakoneta, Ohio, to observe some problems with a pilot run Model 88 tractor. After the customer had

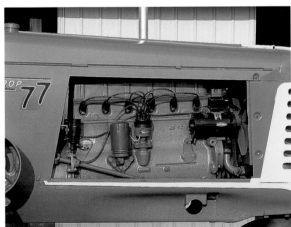

used his PTO a considerable number of hours, the splines were worn off the driveshaft at the flywheel end, and one bull gear in the final drive was worn considerably. It was obvious that the bull gear had been carburized but missed the hardening operation.

Because some late tests indicated that the PTO driveshaft needed to be made from stronger,

OLIVER FACILITIES

The Charles City tractor plant occupied 65 acres, 17 of which were under roof. Throughout its life, it was one of the most modern tractor plants in the world, and the plant underwent many renovations over the years to keep it modern. A good example was the 1948 addition of 100,000 square feet to house a new assembly area, paint system, casting machining, and conveyorized handling of castings from the foundry. The foundry was then remodeled to increase its capacity. This new addition was essential for the production of the new Oliver Fleetline 66, 77, and 88 tractors.

Foundry

The foundry in Charles City was updated several times during its life. The 1948 modernizations provided the extra capacity required to produce the Fleetline tractors and for conveyor belts that took castings from the foundry to the machining area. The foundry was also flexible in providing the necessary varieties of cast iron required in production. One modernization of the foundry added hoods over the casting cooling area of the foundry conveyors to collect the smoke and fumes from the cooling castings, making the foundry one of the cleanest in the world. In fact, the foundry was still one of the most modern when it was closed in 1992.

An electric-powered furnace was installed in the mid-1950s to provide special castings, such as the exhaust manifold, which needed certain alloy additions to control growth under the hot temperatures of the exhaust. The alloy chips from machining steel were used for some of the required alloys. These chips would have burned up in the regular cupola, but they could be loaded into the electric furnace when the furnace was cold and would not burn when the electric power was turned on.

Casting Machining

When the castings cooled, they were removed from the mold and placed on a conveyor. The conveyor transported the castings to a cleaning area where fins, excess sand, and so on were removed. After the castings were cleaned, they were placed again on the conveyor and transported through a primer paint booth and into the next building to the casting machining area. Castings were then removed from the conveyor for machining. After machining, the castings were once again placed on the conveyor and taken to an area where they were included in a subassembly or moved onto the main assembly line. Some of the smaller castings were placed into a skid container and parked near the point in the assembly line where they would be used.

Steel Machining and Stamping

After the 1948 expansion, all steel machining for gears, shafts, axles, and other steel parts was done in the area where the assembly line existed prior to 1948. Steel chips from the machining of alloy gears were saved and used in the foundry's electric furnace.

Also during this time, Oliver developed a highly sophisticated gear manufacturing department. Gears were crown-shaved so that the center of the gear teeth was slightly thicker than the ends of the teeth. Crown-shaving provided for quick wear-in of the gears, resulting in accurate tooth contact with mating gears.

One building was devoted entirely to forming sheet metal for instrument panels, grilles, wheel guards, hoods, and side panels.

New Assembly Line

Also in 1948, the assembly line was conveyorized, which provided smooth movement through the factory of the tractors being assembled. In fact, the assemblers could ride on the conveyor along with each tractor to the point on the line at which their work was done. They could then walk back to their stations and start assembling the next tractor. The speed of the conveyor was based on trying to complete so many tractors per

The Oliver tractor plant at Charles City is shown in this aerial view. Engineering's oval test track is shown in the top center of the photo. Carl Rabe

day. Subassemblies, such as the PTO, pulley, and hydraulics, were delivered to the main assembly line at the points where they were added to the tractor assembly.

Computer Control of Production and Assembly

We started assembling tractors using a computer system with the Supers in 1954. Key-punched cards provided information for parts and assembly. For example, the card would indicate the type of transmission a tractor would receive along with the numbers of parts to be assembled on that tractor. This information was shared across the plant—in the foundry, machine shop, and on the assembly line. Another key-punched card, showing the recommended list price, accompanied each tractor to the dealer.

Painting

Paint companies often said that the quality of paint on Oliver tractors was equal to or higher than the paint on American-made automobiles. The process that allowed such a fine finish began on the main assembly line as the tractor passed through the paint booths. The paint was sprayed from both sides, and both sides had a waterfall curtain that collected excess paint mist. The tractors then entered the oven to bake the paint at a temperature up to 275 degrees F. It was important to adjust the temperature, depending on the size of a tractor and how fast the assembly line traveled. Perishable items, such as batteries and tires, were added to the tractors after leaving the oven.

Tractor Testing

How the early Hart-Parr tractors were tested is not well documented. Apparently, Hart-Parr engineers and dealers observed and researched the needs for tractors and

The tractor assembly line before the 275-degree bake oven. Some parts, such as tires and batteries, did not withstand this high temperature, so they were installed after the bake oven. Carl Rabe

The tires, wheels, and wheel weights were assembled, and then the assemblies were attached to the tractor. These assemblies required cranes to position them on the tractor. Carl Rabe

This photograph of the foundry at the Charles City plant was taken in 1956 by the author's brother-in-law. Harold W. Snyder

The final assembly line was the place where the tires, wheels, batteries, and other low temperature parts were installed. The tractors were then started, the transmission operated, and a general inspection performed. Next they were driven on the rear-wheel power test rollers to make certain that they had the prescribed minimum drawbar power. Carl Rabe

The Oliver tractor test track located at Charles City, Iowa, was similar to the test track at the University of Nebraska at Lincoln. The Oliver test track also had an obstacle course where tractors were driven over logs as shown in the background here. Carl Rabe

Oliver's Hydra-Lectric unit was tested in the experimental engineering laboratories. This cycling test subjected the valves, levers, and electrical connections to continuous up and down operation, giving the hydraulic valves a severe test. Carl Rabe

then attempted to manufacture tractors to meet customer requirements. Testing of the early Oliver models was more elaborate, especially the Model 60, 70, and 80. The testing of the Model 66, 77, and 88 followed some of these established test procedures with many new test procedures added. In the fall of 1944, six prototype tractors of each model were assembled, along with extra component assemblies such as engines, transmissions, differentials, and final drives. Four of these were sent to Arizona where the tractors could be tested in fields for as long as 24 hours per day. Two prototypes of each model were retained in Charles City for local tests by farmers, for laboratory tests, and for redesigning parts as a result of the tests.

Deep plowing in the irrigated Arizona fields required near maximum horsepower, and the 12 prototype tractors were tested there through most of 1945 and then returned to Charles City for disassembly and an evaluation of wear. The prototypes were then updated with redesigned parts and sent to West Farms near Bakersfield, California. West Farms operated approximately 30,000 acres of dry land and irrigated crops. From January through October, we could often test the tractors for 24 hours per day.

Joe Roland was in charge of these tests. He provided a weekly report on the operation of each tractor and other equipment, such as South Bend's Rollover plow. The Rollover plow had right and left plow blades so that a field could be plowed both ways in the same furrow. This type of plow was helpful in maintaining level fields for irrigation. West Farms was used as a testing area until about 1958 when the president of West Farms died.

The next test area was near Lubbock, Texas. The tractors were operated on the plateau where there was much dry land and some irrigated farming. About the same time, some testing was moved to Mississippi. Alva Phelps, the Oliver CEO, had a friend in Mississippi who promised a good testing area, but ultimately neither the Mississippi nor Lubbock areas were satisfactory.

In 1960, we moved Joe Roland and our test equipment back to the Phoenix area. We first worked with the Phoenix Vegetable Company, but we also loaned the test tractors and equipment to anyone in that area who could meet our test requirements. We leased a Quonset hut as headquarters for our equipment and for any repair. This building was located a short distance south of the original Sun City. I usually stayed at the Kings Inn in Sun City when I visited the test areas. I watched Sun City grow during the 1960s. This test area continued to be used as long as Oliver and White Farm Equipment Engineering had a remote testing program.

Tractor tests were also conducted all year near Charles City and elsewhere in the Upper Midwest. Industrial wheel tractors were tested in our laboratory with stress coating and strain gauges. Industrial tractors were also tested anywhere we could find a good application of the tractor and observe its wear.

Tests equivalent to the Nebraska tests were conducted on the Fleetline models on the streets near the plant and in the dynamometer laboratory. Later, a test track was built on Oliver's property in Charles City. The outer track was constructed to be comparable to the Nebraska test track. The inner track included an obstacle course with logs bolted to the concrete. The purpose of the obstacle course was to determine which parts of the tractor were subject to early fatigue failure. Test tractors and equipment rolling over the logs at different speeds caused shock load conditions.

Engine and Transmission Testing

Engines underwent numerous tests. Before the introduction of the latest oil bath and dry type air cleaners, most tractor companies had a "dust room" where an engine could run continuously under load in a controlled dusty atmosphere. At Oliver, the dust was brought in from Arizona. The wear areas in the engine were measured before and after each test. The purpose of the test was to determine the most efficient air cleaner for each model of engine.

Engines were also tested on a dynamometer with a direct hookup or on a belt-driven dynamometer. Engine power and fuel consumption were measured with each combination of parts, such as different combinations of intake manifolds, air cleaners, radiators, and other engine parts. The purpose of this test was to establish the most practical combination to provide long life and low fuel consumption. It was not unusual for an engine to be tested for 2,000 to 3,000 dynamometer hours to arrive at the best combination of parts.

The transmission, differential, and final drive, including the axles, was an extremely important assembly. Consequently, they underwent some of the most rigorous testing. One test, called a "four-square" test, used two units opposing each other. A tractor engine does its work by applying a rotating force on the transmission shaft. The four-square test used two transmissions, differentials, and final drives, and a large sprocket fastened to each axle with a large roller chain connecting the sprockets on each side. The transmission input shafts were rotated in opposite directions until the equivalent force of the engine was reached. The two input shafts were then fastened to provide the desired rotating force or torque. Then, it was only necessary to rotate the input shafts at the engine's governed speed. The four-square test was especially severe because the test torque was established at full engine power, while the average load in the field only utilized about 55 percent of the available engine power.

We attempted to judge how a tractor would be used and determined an average percentage of operation for each of the six transmission speeds. We then tested the units in each speed according to the estimated percentage of time it would spend in that speed for a total of 1,000 hours. There were frequent inspections to observe and measure wear patterns. The lowest speeds were discounted to some degree because the wheels would spin out before there was enough traction to use all of the engine's power. Some of the higher speeds used the same transmission gears as other speeds so that the road speed was not an important factor in determining the final design of the gears.

Laboratory tests were also conducted on other individual assemblies, such as the pulley, power take-off, and hydraulics. The pulley with the link attached rotated slowly. Each revolution of the pulley completed a cycle of the Hydra-Lectric cylinder. The cycle provided continuous lifting and lowering of the tractor front frame and engine. When the load was lifted, the unit would stop momentarily, and then the valve would open to lower the load. The test unit was operated at near full pressure for 1,000 hours or more. Some parts were redesigned as a result of this test.

This test was quite severe compared to actual field operation. First, use in the field required infrequent actuation of the hydraulic system. Second, average actuations required only 30 to 50 percent of the available pressure. The life of the hydraulic system under these normal conditions would be several times the life of a unit operated under the severe laboratory conditions. Brakes were also cycled with a Hydra-Lectric system to actuate the brakes frequently.

These are just a few examples of the hundreds of tests conducted in the laboratory and in the fields. Charlie Adams, a member of our experimental engineering department, had experience with the University of Nebraska's tractor test laboratories before coming to Oliver. He was an expert at designing special tests. He was slow and methodical. We had brainstorming sessions to design tests that would help us overcome field problems. If we asked him for a commitment on when a test could start, he was vague. But with some help from us, we would set a target date. Charlie nearly always completed his part of the assignment ahead of schedule.

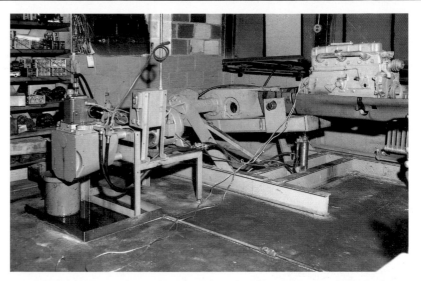

The Hydra-Lectric cylinder was operated at maximum hydraulic oil pressure, lifting a weight equivalent to that of the tractor. This was a severe test because the required amount of hydraulic oil pressure under normal operation was only a quarter of the maximum, and the test subjected the cylinder to rapid cycling where normal use would only require intermittent lifting. Carl Rabe

Another typical example of laboratory tests was the one using the Hydra-Lectric as a means to test the brake bands. The rapid cycling of the brake bands increased the temperature so much that it caused the brake lining to fail. Carl Rabe

highly heat-treated steel to avoid wear, we began experimenting with 4140 steel. We used electrical induction to harden the splined areas and the smaller part of the driveshaft that passed through the tubular clutch and transmission shafts. I called the plant at Charles City and asked that a new induction-hardened driveshaft, a new induction-hardened flywheel hub with splines, and a new bull gear be shipped as quickly as possible. These were sent at no charge to the dealer or the customer, and Oliver reimbursed the dealer for his mechanic's time to install the new parts. Oliver established a service program to replace all the PTO driveshafts and flywheel hubs in the pilot run Model 88s.

Engaging the independent PTO clutch quickly with the throttle wide open could cause some extreme shock loads on the PTO. With the old transmission-driven PTO, the operator would feel the shock shudder through his body. My solution was to mount the PTO clutch lever on the left side of the operator's seat and provide operation guidelines. The operators were advised to reduce the engine speed, engage the PTO clutch slowly, and then increase the engine speed. This way both hands could be used to coordinate the PTO engagement without undue shock loads on the shafts and mechanism.

The new Oliver Hydra-Lectric hydraulic lift was a major innovation of the Fleetline series. It allowed an operator to change the working depth at which his implements were operating without stopping to get off the tractor. Here is a Hydra-Lectric hydraulic lift on a 1950 Row Crop 77.

RIGHT: Early Fleetline tractors such as this 1949 Row Crop 77 used this mechanical power lift, a standard piece of equipment that was designed for Hart-Parr and Oliver tractors with front-mounted equipment. A hydraulic lift became available as an option in 1950.

FAR RIGHT: The Hydra-Lectric hydraulic cylinder mounted on the implement. Early versions were controlled by the two switches mounted to the left-hand side of the steering column.

The pilot run Model 88s all had the PTO lever on the left side, but because of a deluge of customer requests, the lever was moved to the right side. Moving the lever to the right side may have contributed to failures of either the driveshaft or the standard output shaft. Such a location prompted the operator to increase the engine speed to maximum with the right hand and then quickly engage the PTO with the same right hand. We measured shock loads on the driveshaft and standard output shaft equal to 10 times the continuous output of the 88 engine.

The next step was to experiment with various PTO clutch spring pressures. We knew that the high shock load occurred only for a fraction of a second until the clutch could break loose and slip, so we established our clutch spring pressure at only 1.25 times the maximum power of a Model 88 engine. The trade-off with such a design was that we anticipated more PTO clutch plate failures. The clutch problems, however, were not too many considering the large number of tractors and all of the available implements. Also, as time went on, the operators became more aware of the need for smooth engagement of the PTO clutch.

The Oliver independent PTO became the envy of most tractor manufacturers. Within a few years, most agricultural tractor companies in the world had designed implements for the independent PTO, at least on the larger tractors.

I represented Oliver's tractor division in the Farm and Industrial Equipment Institute (FIEI). After an FIEI meeting in 1954, Ed Tanquary, staff engineer for International Harvester and chairman of the FIEI Advisory Engineering Committee, and I continued to discuss the day's activities and where we were going on PTO standards.

I asked him, "Is IHC concerned about the independent PTO or do you think Oliver is too small to be a factor in their total tractor sales?"

He seemed to be startled by my question and said, "You will never know how much Oliver's independent PTO concerns our company."

Then I said, "Oliver has had the independent PTO for six years. Why doesn't IHC have it yet?"

His answer was, "We are so big and there are so many levels of management that by the time a proposal reaches the top and gets back to the responsible design people, it is often obsolete and we have to start all over again. We are envious of you. You can prepare a proposal, send it to your Chicago office, and within

a few days you have the approval to go ahead with the proposal. If IHC had your tractors with our sales department and Oliver had our tractors with your sales department, we would do extremely well and you would soon go broke. Your sales department is expecting you to keep providing something new so that the tractors will sell themselves. Your sales department has forgotten how to hard-sell farm equipment."

I wrote a paper on the development of the PTO for agricultural equipment titled, "The Development of Agricultural Equipment Power Take-off Mechanism," and presented it in Milwaukee, Wisconsin, at the Society of Automotive Engineers (SAE) Farm and Construction Machinery Technical Meeting in September 1980. This paper was reprinted in the SP-470 book published in 1981 for the celebration of the SAE's 75th anniversary.

A few product liability lawsuits were filed against Oliver involving the PTO. The following case is related without names. This case involved a 77 Standard tractor in South Dakota that was manufactured in 1950 and was nearly 18 years old when the accident occurred on March 4, 1968.

One of Oliver's many innovations was to develop the first practical diesel tractor. By 1954, Oliver sold approximately 54 percent of all diesel agricultural tractors. This "Diesel Power" decal was seen on the early 66, 77, and 88 diesel tractors. The first Fleetline tractors also had an American Bosch single-plunger fuel-injection pump, but the control linkage failed on some units. It was redesigned by American Bosch and such failures were avoided. All tractors with the old controls were changed. The Bosch pumps were soon replaced with the Roosa single-plunger fuel-injection pump. Invented by Vernon Roosa, this simple pump cost less but performed as well or better, and was Oliver's choice for its later diesel engines.

Oliver extensively tested and developed the Fleetline tractors, with prototypes constructed as early as 1944. The first experimental and pilot-run Fleetline tractors were made with the old styling to test the mechanical aspects and to keep the new styling a secret until the line was introduced. This 1947 Row Crop 88 was one of the pilot run models built with the old Model 60 styling. Regular production began in 1948.

Early failure of the rear hub on prototype Model 88s caused Oliver to switch to a malleable cast-iron axle and to use an axle hub with three U-bolts. There were no more failures of these hubs. To provide better traction, Oliver used steel rims attached with bolted lugs to cast-iron wheels.

The owner filled a DuAll silage wagon from his silo. He then drove the tractor and wagon to his livestock feed bunks. The wagon was unloaded by engaging the PTO. The wagon mechanism moved the silage forward to a beater, a rotating mechanism with large spikes. The beater forced the silage through an opening onto a cross conveyor, which then deposited the silage into the livestock feed bunk. When the owner emptied the silage into the bunks, he noticed some clumps of frozen silage lodged in the wagon. He disengaged the PTO and climbed into the wagon to dislodge the frozen clumps of silage. He claimed that the tractor PTO engaged itself and drew him into the beater where he suffered severe injury to one leg and some injury to the other leg. Other claims in the case were that the PTO control mechanism was not fail-

This is a 1947 Row Crop 88, shown here with a three-bottom plow. The first 1,300 Row Crop and 685 Standard Oliver 88 tractors used the old-style sheet metal.

safe and that there should have been an automatic safety release to prevent injury.

Oliver purchased a used 77 Standard from the same area in South Dakota that was the same age as the one involved in the accident. In fact, they were only a few serial numbers apart. The attorneys managed to buy the DuAll wagon involved in the accident. The tractor and the silage wagon were taken to Naperville, Illinois, for testing and evaluation.

The main claim by the plaintiff was that the PTO control system was not fail-safe. To prevent accidental clutch engagement, the PTO clutch lever did have an automatic lockout when the PTO clutch was disengaged. The pawl on the lever engaged an adjustable stop on the clutch cover. The PTO had an over-center clutch with heavy spring pressure behind it. When the PTO clutch was disengaged, the control lever snapped rearward and its pawl locked up against its adjustable stop. To engage the PTO, the operator had to push down on a gearshift-type knob at the top

of the control lever to lower the pawl below its stop and then push the lever forward past the over-center position. The clutch then stayed engaged until the lever was pulled rearward to disengage the clutch.

The Model 77 and 88 PTO clutch had double-disc friction plates with a center plate between them. Three small separating springs were held between the front and rear pressure plates of the

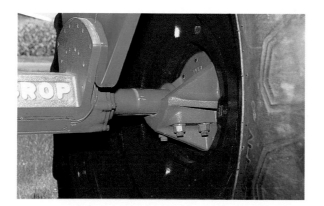

These pilot-run 88s were equipped with independent PTOs. The steel on the rear axles of the Fleetline tractors was hardened on the surface by heating with electric current, called induction hardening. This provided a more satisfactory axle and solved a number of problems in which rear axles had failed under heavy loads.

clutch. These three springs passed through holes in lugs of the center plate to separate the clutch plates and the center plate. The separation of the discs and the center plate was important to prevent any drag or rotation of the PTO output shaft when the clutch was disengaged.

I was among the expert witnesses who traveled to South Dakota to view the tractor involved in the accident. We obtained permission to disassemble the PTO clutch and photograph the parts. We discovered that the three separating springs were missing and the holes in the center plate and the front and rear pressure plates were filled with grease and particles from wearing of the clutch face. Also, the clutch control lever was adjusted tightly. Possibly, this was done by the owner to disengage the PTO and prevent any drag by the clutch parts. This led us to assume that the owner had done his own service repair on his 77 Standard PTO. The result was that the clutch was modified and a condition was created that would permit some drag of the clutch parts when the clutch was disengaged.

In tests conducted on the tractor and the silage wagon at Naperville we learned that when the three separating springs were omitted, approximately 1/4 horsepower drag could be obtained by the clutch parts. This drag was enough to cause serious damage to a board fed into the silage wagon's beater. Fifteen horsepower was required to unload silage from the DuAll wagon—approximately 60 times the power that would cause injury to a human being. This much power could not feasibly be shut off suddenly in a way to prevent injury, as asserted in the case.

We toured all of the farm buildings while we were at the owner's farm. In one garage there were many modified Oliver PTO parts. Some of these included sintered metal clutch plate facings. Sintered metal clutch facings were not practical for this application because the coefficient of friction was much lower than the non-metallic production and repair friction plates. We also noted some worn PTO clutch release bearings. These had apparently failed because of the owner's attempt to use the release bearing alone to prevent clutch drag after the separating springs were removed.

Another concern was where the owner got the tractor. We contacted the Oliver dealer who worked with this owner and got permission to review his sales and service records. The previous dealer had died about two years before the accident, but the appropriate records had been transferred to the new dealership.

We learned that the owner had previously purchased as many as six Oliver tractors from the local dealership, the latest of which was an 88 tractor that had the same PTO, except for a longer driveshaft. While there were service invoices for PTO repair on this Model 88 and repairs on all of the other tractors, there were none for the 77 Standard. Why were there sales and service repair invoices on all of the other Oliver tractors but none relating to the 77 Standard?

We checked sales records at the Charles City plant and found that this tractor, when new, was shipped to the Kansas City sales branch. How did the tractor get from Kansas City to South Dakota? These questions might have been answered if the case had been tried in court, but it was settled out of court for a sum of money that should take care of the injured man for the rest of his life.

Before it was settled, however, and in preparation for the trial, I was assigned to locate and inspect at least 25 Model 77 and 88 tractors within a 50-mile radius of Chicago. My purpose was to evaluate the condition of the PTO control mechanism from many standpoints, such as adjustment and clutch drag. I called all the Oliver dealers to find out if they had any Model 77 and 88 tractors in their inventory. I was amazed to find that only two tractors were in the dealers' inventories and one was to be delivered to a buyer the next day. I asked what happened to used Model 77 and 88 tractors. The general answer was that farmers don't trade them. They keep them for their second tractor or put a loader on them and use them for chores. The few that are traded are sold quickly from the used-tractor inventory.

I surveyed 42 Oliver 77 and 88 tractors, all of which were 15 to 21 years old. I found only four tractors with PTO control mechanisms in poor condition. Repair parts were sent to the dealers for these tractors. Fifteen tractors were rated "fair" because they needed adjustment of the pawl to the stop, the hand knob on top of the lever was missing, or there were other minor maintenance needs. Many of these tractors were adjusted at the time of my visit. The other 23 tractors

had good maintenance and were in good operating condition. When one considers the age of these tractors and their general usage, I felt that the PTO control mechanism had proven to be very good.

The visits to these Model 77 and 88 tractors gave me an opportunity to visit with many customers to ask some questions. Why did they keep these old Oliver tractors? The most common answer was because of the independent PTO. They also mentioned the smooth-running six-cylinder engines, easy ride seat, and the automatic Hydra-Lectric hydraulic system.

Belt Pulley Design

I designed the belt pulley when I had some spare time during the PTO project. One design criterion was that it be a special unit that could be added or removed easily, so I designed a pulley that could be removed from the flanged shaft by four capscrews from the outside, leaving no projection outside the sheet metal outline. The belt pulley housing was to be mounted on the front of the rear frame. Some changes to the main frame foundry casting patterns were required to add bosses for the belt pulley housing mounting. An oil trough was also added to feed oil to and from the transmission for adequate lubrication of the pulley mechanism and for cooling the oil.

This specification sheet for the Oliver Standard 88 features the new Ridemaster Seat, a feature that was part of increasing awareness of the importance of operator comfort.
Floyd County Historical Society

Throughout the development of Oliver tractors, the standard configuration continued to be offered. This 1947 Standard 88 is an early Fleetline tractor.

The Model 77 and 88 had a provision for a multiple reverse transmission to provide four forward speeds and four reverse speeds. This option was used primarily for the northwest United States where pea harvesters were mounted on the tractors. The pulley housing had to be designed so that it would not interfere with a special shaft bracket or a cover when there was no multiple reverse idler shaft. But as the industry developed larger and higher-capacity self-propelled pea harvesters, this option was no longer needed on our tractors.

Overall, the belt pulley was successful and had little or no serious service problems. Since that time, most of the belt-driven equipment, such as threshers, has been replaced by self-propelled or PTO-driven machinery.

Hydra-Lectric Implement Power Lifts

A mechanical implement power lift was developed for the first Hart-Parr and Oliver Row Crop tractors. It was controlled by a foot pedal located on the right side of the unit. One actuation of the pedal resulted in a one-half revolution of the cross shaft, which had an arm attached to each end and provided for both left and right lifting and lowering of the implement. If the implement was in its

working position, actuation of the pedal raised it to its non-working, or transport, position. A second actuation of the pedal rotated the shaft another half a revolution, which returned the implement to its working position.

The growth in the agricultural equipment industry during the 1930s and early 1940s prompted the tractor industry to consider lifting and lowering of implements by hydraulic power. John Deere was one of the first companies to introduce hydraulic power lifts. On the Deere units, the working depth of towed or mounted equipment could not be changed easily from the tractor seat when the automatic shut-off at each end of the cylinder stroke was pre-set. So, to avoid getting down each time, one had to forgo the automatic shutoff and manually set the working depth each time the implement was lowered into its working position.

Oliver's design criteria included an automatic shutoff of the hydraulic cylinder lift and lower functions and a simple means of changing the working depth from the operator's seat while the tractor and implement continued in motion. When the hydraulic control lever was moved to the lift position, it was held by a detent until the hydraulic cylinder reached the extended position, and then the control lever automatically returned to neutral. Also, when the control lever was moved to the lower position, the control lever was held by a detent until the pre-set implement working depth was reached. Then a valve on the cylinder cut off the flow of oil to the hydraulic cylinder and the control lever automatically returned to neutral.

The Oliver Hydra-Lectric was controlled by three-way electrical circuits. Changing the working depth on the go was easy to do. This was accomplished by moving the hydraulic control lever sideways to energize the magnet on the Hydra-Lectric hydraulic cylinder. When the control lever was moved sideways and then in the lower position, the cylinder collar pushed on the cylinder rod to change its pre-set position. This resulted in increased working depth of the implement. If the operator wanted to decrease the implement working depth, the control lever was moved sideways and then in the lift direction. The electric magnet held the collar and slid it on the cylinder rod until a new working depth was established. When the implement was raised to the transport position, the Hydra-Lectric cylinder was completely extended.

The operator didn't have to set the implement working depth by observing the cylinder and manually controlling the working depth each time the implement was raised. Instead, the operator could change the working depth by nudging the control lever to change the position of the collar on the cylinder rod. The Oliver Hydra-Lectric was the most automatic and versatile hydraulic system on any agricultural equipment.

The first electrical switches for the Hydra-Lectric were small toggle levers mounted on the steering column. We made an attempt to seal the switches so that the electrical contact points would be protected from the weather. But temperature changes, rain, fertilizer, and other factors caused the seals to break down and the switches to malfunction early in the warranty period. The solution was to put the Hydra-Lectric unit below the instrument panel with the electrical switches inside the oil reservoir where they were covered with oil. The oil protected the switch contact points and prevented them from corroding and malfunctioning.

Electrical cord ends also corroded and malfunctioned, unless they were properly maintained. The electrical cord between the unit and the breakaway hydraulic coupling area, and the cord to the Hydra-Lectric hydraulic cylinder, had specially molded rubber ends to protect them from the weather. Still, this was not a perfect solution. Much study has been devoted to these corrosion problems by companies making lawn care and skid steer loader products, but I am not aware of any design that provides long-term success for sealing against all ambient and weather elements.

During the patent search for the Hydra-Lectric system, we learned that Bendix Aviation Division in North Hollywood, California, had a patent on a hydraulic cylinder controlled by electrical circuits. So Oliver initially worked with Bendix to manufacture its first Hydra-Lectric hydraulic cylinders, but there were quality problems. Oliver's warranty cost was too great and the Hydra-Lectric system was poorly accepted at first.

Oliver engineering suggested many changes to improve the quality, but Bendix was slow in responding. In March 1951 we discontinued the manufacture of Oliver's hydraulic cylinder by Bendix. Oliver engineering made its own detail drawings with changes to improve the quality.

Some of Oliver's industrial engineering and manufacturing supervisors were skeptical that Oliver could machine to such close tolerances. But Plant Manager George Bird said, "We are going to manufacture our own hydraulic cylinders. It is up to you fellows to get the job done."

Oliver's manufacture of its own Hydra-Lectric cylinder solved many problems. Oliver received Patent No. 2,707,867 on the system. This patent was issued in 1955 to Charles A. L. Ruhl and assigned to Oliver. It was one of the most complicated patents on hydraulics.

But there were still corrosion problems. Customers who did not maintain the unit properly were very critical of it. Also, competitors, who were prevented from using the same system covered by Oliver's patent, were vocal to potential customers about the corrosion problems. Finally, these problems caused Oliver to offer an optional hydraulic system with manual control that was comparable to competitors' hydraulic systems. The Hydra-Lectric system was still used, however, and rated excellent by those customers who maintained their units well.

Transmission and Final Drive

The Fleetline 66, 77, and 88 had basic four-speed (three forward and one reverse) transmissions. The input shaft and counter shaft system provided for doubling the available speeds to six forward and two reverse. The original design of the differential spiral bevel gear and pinion offered some flexibility, which allowed the differential to support all of the speeds.

Row Crop tractors were designed to have a top speed of about 12 miles per hour. Since the Row Crop tractors had a high center of gravity, safe execution of turns was a major consideration in determin-

The Model 88 pilot run tractors and first production 77s and 88s until January 1949 were made with the power take-off (PTO) lever on the left side so that the operator could use two hands to reduce the engine speed and engage the PTO properly. The mechanical power lift, clutch pedal, and equalizer brake pedals are also shown here. *Carl Rabe*

Independent power take-off (PTO) was one of Oliver's most important innovations. Although it first was introduced by Hart-Parr in 1928, the advantages were not clear at that time. Oliver offered a practical independent PTO on the new Fleetline tractors. The initial design with the PTO lever on the left was not accepted by operators, so the tractors had the PTO lever on the right, as shown here in 1949.

Equalizer brake pedals were offered on the Fleetline series. This allowed the operator to brake only the right or left rear wheel to aid in turning the tractor. The band brakes used on the Fleetline tractors were less effective when the tractor was going in reverse and had some experimental failures. This led Oliver to contact brake companies and adapt the new double-disc brakes to the Fleetlines. Band brakes were used on the 66, 77, and 88 production tractors until 1951.

ing the maximum speed. On two occasions, our experimental tractor test drivers turned sharply at road speed and the tricycle-type tractors rolled over. Fortunately, both drivers were thrown clear of the tractor and were not seriously hurt. Consequently, Oliver maintained a limit on the maximum speed in sixth gear, the road gear. The adjustable front axle Row Crop tractors were somewhat more stable.

The Standard tractor had a lower center of gravity and limited oscillation of the front axle. There was no Standard tricycle type. This allowed for a higher road speed of about 18 miles per hour.

One interesting problem developed between the experimental Model 88 tractors and the pilot run. Some tractors would not stay in fifth gear while pulling a load requiring most of the tractor's power. The experimental tractors had tight-fitting splines of the small pinion on the spiral bevel pinion transmission output shaft. These pinions were made on a production basis for the pilot run, and the heat treating caused some of the pinions to enlarge in the spline area. I went to Le Mars, Iowa, the site of the test, and exchanged the fifth-gear pinion with a more tightly fitting pinion on the output shaft.

Experimental engineering set up a transmission with an opening on the top to view the transmission gears. Then a load was applied to the axle. One suggestion to keep the transmission in gear was to provide a heavier detent to hold the shifter rod from moving out of gear, but that option would not work because we could not keep the fifth pinion from moving out of mesh with the large countershaft gear even with a 6-foot bar. Also ,the shifter fork got so hot from the friction that smoke appeared. I made a force diagram and some calculations. The fifth-gear pinion was removed and the tool room ground the spline from the pinion, leaving only the splines under the large countershaft gear teeth. This revised fifth pinion was then installed in the test transmission. This solved the problem; we could not pry the pinion out of mesh with the 6-foot bar. Oliver's service department created a replacement program for any tractors with the fifth-gear problem.

This experience prompted a review of all the transmission gears on the Model 66, 77, and 88. Through this review we discovered that the double sliding gear on the input shaft could cause some similar problems. To avoid the same problem, the involute splines under the shifter fork groove were eliminated.

The splines and the gear mesh were then compatible, avoiding any tendency for the gear to come out of mesh. These changes were then made to all of the comparable gears in the Model 66, 77, and 88 tractor transmissions.

We also designed an interlock to prevent shifting two gearshift rods at once, which would cause a gear lock-up. Still, the gears did lock up under some conditions. This actually occurred with some of the experimental tractors in the Phoenix area. To understand this problem, we laid out a 20:1 scale drawing to show the movement of the gearshift lever, the interlock, and the three gearshift rods. What we learned from this layout led to the decision to make steel stampings and locate the locking lugs accurately on the stamping. We made this change for the Fleetline production run. I am not aware of any gearshift lock-up problems on the Fleetline production tractors.

Another feature on the Model 77 and 88 tractors was the multiple reverse transmission, which allowed special equipment to be mounted on the rear of the tractor and the tractor to be driven in reverse. This special equipment was primarily for harvesting vegetables such as peas. An idler gear and shaft were added to the front of the transmission and four speeds forward and four speeds in reverse were available. This provided a reasonable road speed in either direction. Oliver never sold a large quantity of tractors with the multiple reverse transmission. At the same time we were introducing the Fleetline tractors, local manufacturers in the Pacific Northwest were designing larger self-propelled vegetable harvesters.

The Thomas Varidraulic Drive was another option on the Fleetline tractors that did not sell well. This drive mechanism had a fluid coupling with variable space between the stator and the rotor that was controlled by the operator. Slow speeds were achieved by increasing the distance between the stator and rotor of the fluid coupling. Maximum speed was reached by reducing the distance between the stator and rotor of the fluid coupling. This fluid coupling was very inefficient, and slow speeds were difficult to control. I recall driving a tractor with this variable fluid coupling. I started with the brakes set lightly to simulate a small drawbar pull requirement. I moved the control slowly toward the maximum speed. Suddenly, the tractor lurched forward. This was quite impractical. I do not recall that we sold any tractors with the Thomas Varidraulic Drive. If any were sold, the application had to be special.

This 1949 Standard 88 has the new Fleetline styling. A Standard 88 tested at Nebraska in late 1947 and early 1948 produced 29.08 drawbar and 40.96 belt horsepower. The tractor weighed in at 4,863 pounds.

Lights were mounted on the wheel guards, as shown on this Row Crop 88. Lights failed on the experimental Fleetline tractors because the wires were torn loose in the field. To prevent this from occurring, the wires were run through steel tubes attached to the wheel guard and the axle housing.

Sound Reduction

One of Oliver's goals with the Fleetline tractors was to limit sound levels to 85 decibels at the operator's ear. This goal was accomplished on the experimental tractors, but it was harder to accomplish on the production run tractors. To accomplish this goal, the transmission parts were made with tighter tolerances than in the past. Some parts had to be honed to fit their mating parts, such as gears to their shafts. The transmissions were the spur gear type, which means that the gear teeth were parallel to the shaft, resulting in quiet transmissions on all three prototypes. Engine mufflers were also selected to maximize quietness.

The pilot runs of 300 of each model tractor made more transmission noise than the experimental prototypes. The gears were looser on the shafts and not as accurately machined. For the production tractors, we selected a louder engine muffler to place the

Industrial 88s were built from 1947 to 1954. This is a 1947 Industrial 88. Buyers could retrofit the new bodywork to the 1947 pilot run Model 88s.

gear noise more in the background. Helical gear transmissions were originally considered, but the cost was too great.

When we started research on quieter transmissions, we wanted to determine the source of the noise and the frequencies (vibrations per second) that made up the noise. One Saturday, when the plant was closed and quiet, Tony Obermeier and I conducted a sound test. I had a Melody saxophone in the key of C and could relate the frequencies by harmonizing with the transmission sound. Tony ran the tractor on the inspection treadmill while I scanned the notes on the saxophone. We thought that the main frequency would be the same as the number of teeth in mesh per second between the input gear and its mating gear on the countershaft. I found it easy to harmonize with the main frequency. The remaining frequencies were generated by the engine, other gear combinations, and other functions of the tractor.

To continue our research, we sought a consultant who was experienced with reducing noise in commercial products. We hired Silencing Consultants of America of Toledo, Ohio, which had been successful in reducing the noise of paper-making machines and was also doing some consulting work for Caterpillar. In August 1949, we signed a contract with Silencing Consultants of America for a special noise analysis of our tractors.

We sent a Model 77 tractor to Toledo for the evaluations. Mori, an engineer with Silencing Consultants, had a special treadmill made so he could operate the tractor in each gear. He became confused when he changed gears and found as many as eight new frequencies. He ignored our suggestion to consider the frequencies being equal to the number of teeth in mesh per second. Ultimately, the data he gave us were within the variability of his equipment, and his conclusions were false. We were running out of funds for the contract during early March 1950, so we gave notice that the project would be canceled as soon as certain data were obtained.

We brought the Model 77 tractor back to Charles City and purchased a high-quality tape recorder, sound analyzer, frequency oscillator, and other equipment to do our own sound analysis. The results of these tests revealed that spur gear noise could be reduced by more accurately machining and fitting the gears. It was amazing how much the sound was reduced after the transmissions were worn in. We started crown-shaving the gears in about 1950, which assisted in a quick wear-in of the transmissions.

Axles and Hubs

At the start of Fleetline tractor production, Oliver used a high-grade alloy steel (A-4140) for rear axles. After machining, the axles were completely hardened to approximately 340 Brinell hardness. This material and heat treatment was a common selection for axles in the tractor industry and had been used quite successfully in the older 60, 70, and 80 models.

During the late 1940s, the harvesting products plant in Battle Creek developed a two-row corn picker to mount on the Model 77 and 88 tractors. These pickers were excellent and created much enthusiasm among Oliver dealers and customers. The next year it was full speed ahead for the manufacture of the Oliver #4 mounted corn picker.

A pilot run of approximately 50 #4 mounted corn pickers was sold to owners of 77 and 88 tractors in the Corn Belt. Customers with large fields of corn were chosen wherever possible to get as much usage as possible. Also, the farms that received a pilot unit were carefully chosen so that a representative from Oliver could follow each unit.

Some rear-axle failures occurred on the 77 when the #4 picker was installed. Oliver's evaluation revealed that the rear-axle failures did not occur in the fields but on roads, especially gravel roads with a rough, washboard-like surface. The early failures were on 77 tractors owned by custom operators who picked corn for neighbors and then drove over rough roads at maximum speed to the next field. The rough roads caused some high shock loads on the rear axle.

A failed rear axle was sent to Charles City for evaluation. We noted that there were scratches on the curved part between the anti-friction bearing surface and the larger part of the axle. The failure was typical of bending fatigue.

The Charles City engineering department, with the assistance of Oliver's metallurgists and industrial engineers, brainstormed about the situation. First, we needed a severe test whereby we could cause a quick failure of a 77 production rear axle. We would then use this same test for any proposed solution. A test was built that was capable of adding a weight severity factor of one and one-half that of the tractor and the picker together. We also drove the axle at the speed of an electric motor as another severity factor. If an axle on a 77 tractor was driven at this high speed, it would be traveling about 140 miles per hour.

Second, we needed to provide a smooth radius, which located the outer axle bearing to a shoulder backed by the larger part of the axle. Scratches on the surface of a radius of this type will tend to cause early failure. While we were testing a production axle to establish a base for comparison, we rolled the radius to locate the outer axle bearing. The purpose was to remove any machine scratches on the test axle.

The first failure was on the tapered outer axle bearing. The severity factors had exceeded the deflection permissible for such a bearing, so we substituted a barrel roller-type outer axle bearing that would tolerate more deflection or misalignment. Production axles then failed consistently after about four hours of test operation.

The axle with the smooth radius, which located the outer bearing, showed some improvement over the production axle, but this was not yet an ade-

quate solution. Our goal was to find an axle that would pass our severe test without failure after four million revolutions in the test. Metallurgists had determined that if a part had undergone four million bending cycles without failure, the part would not fail unless the load on the part was increased.

The Oliver metallurgists at Charles City were already working with induction-hardening equipment for large parts such as axles. Induction hardening is a process whereby high-frequency electricity is applied to heat-selected areas of a part. When the part is cooled quickly, the hot areas become hard. We asked for engineering representatives of steel companies to meet with us. We selected a medium carbon steel (C-1038) and then induction-hardened the outside diameter of the axle to approximately 3/16 of an inch deep. The outer and inner ends were then ground to size to fit the outer and inner bearings.

These axles did not fail under severe test conditions. We began making replacement axles from C-1038 induction-hardened steel within a few days, with the cooperation of our metallurgists, the steel companies, bearing companies, our industrial engineering staff, and our machine shop.

The service department offered the new axles free to customers with a 77 tractor and #4

The pilot run of Fleetline tractors included standard and industrial models. This 1947 Industrial 88 bears serial number 1. The industrial tractors had their own separate serial numbers.

picker. We also paid a labor allowance for the time to exchange the axles.

The benefit of this whole program is that we solved the problem and reduced the cost of each tractor significantly by changing from the A-4140 to the C-1038 steel for the axles. The solution to this problem is an excellent example of problems becoming the mother of invention. Where there is no problem, we tend to continue in the same way.

The rear-axle hub on the experimental tractors had a wedge-shaped projection that fit tightly into a wedge-shaped groove in the axle. Two U-bolts wrapped around the axle and then passed through holes in the hub. The U-bolts were to draw in and lock the projection on the hub into the groove of the axle. The experimental hubs were carefully machined by hand. There were no hub failures on the experimental tractors, but in late 1945 and early 1946 the pilot run of 88s had a few hub failures that occurred a few weeks before the start of the first 88 production run. We decided to make the hubs of malleable casting instead of the regular high-strength cast iron. Some of these tractors had malleable cast rear-axle hubs. These could be identified by the thinner flange and other areas of the casting.

Oliver engineering searched for and found a test to cause a cast-iron hub to quickly fail. A movie camera was used to film the end of the axle and the hub during the test. The film showed that just before the failure occurred, the hub separated from the axle in the vicinity of the wedge-locking key between the axle and the hub. We then tested a malleable cast-iron hub. It was an improvement over the regular casting hub but not enough of one to assure us that it was the answer to hub breakage.

We brainstormed about the situation and all engineers involved agreed that if we clamped the hub and axle together tightly enough, there would be no separation during these high-shock loads and the cast-iron hub would not fail. We decided to try three U-bolts instead of two. The addition of the extra U-bolt was tested, and we had no failures during the severe shock loads. Incidentally, these tests were conducted with a remote tractor ignition shut-off, not an operator in the seat, because the safety of the operator was most important. To our knowledge, there were few, if any, hub failures with the three U-bolts tightened to engineering's specifications.

Wheels

Steel wheels were purchased from Electric Wheel Company of Quincy, Illinois. The steel wheels were manufactured in two parts—a disc welded to a rim. The tread adjustment was limited but quite satisfactory for most applications. For higher traction requirements, such as for Row Crop tractors, Oliver manufactured cast-iron wheels that provided additional weight for traction and that were machined to provide many adjustments for tread width. The rim was separate from the wheel, with formed ridges that were offset from the center line of the rim on the inside diameter. The separate offset rim with the cast-iron wheel and straight adjustable axle provided for great tread adjustment. The steel rim was attached to the wheel by positioning the rim on the cast-iron wheel and then using bolted lugs to hold the rim ridge tightly on the wheel.

Brakes

The Oliver Model 60 tractor had an equalizer brake pedal system designed by Milford D. Stewart. He received a patent on the system (#2,443,331), which was assigned to Oliver. The left and right brake pedals were located above the transmission and could

be operated by the right or left foot. A bar was attached to both brake pedals with a pad in the center. The operator could assist tractor steering by putting pressure on one brake pedal at a time. Pressure on the right pedal assisted in right turns, and pressure on the left pedal assisted in making left turns. Pressure on the pad of the equalizer bar set both brakes to stop the tractor. This brake control system was so successful that it was used on the new Fleetline models.

The experimental, pilot runs, and first production runs of the Fleetline 66, 77, and 88 tractors had a band brake that had been used successfully on the Oliver Model 60 tractors. It was self-energized in the forward direction. That is, when either the right or left brake was engaged, while the tractor moved forward, the band would wrap tightly around the drum and add to the braking capacity. The disadvantage of this brake was that it was less effective in reverse. Consequently, some failed and we received complaints about the lack of braking capacity in reverse.

To remedy this, we tried anchoring the brake band by a lug on the band that fit into a slot on the rear main frame and brake cover. This provided some effect on braking in both forward and reverse. About

this time, I was traveling with a young New Jersey territory manager by the name of Dutch Zandbergen. We stopped to see a tomato farmer who had brake problems and found him in the middle of a large tomato field. Dutch introduced me and said to the farmer, "You said that you would like to get your hands on an engineer from the factory, and here he is." He jumped off the tractor, started swearing at me, lost his hat in the wind, and yelled at his son to retrieve his hat.

The tomato farmer used his brakes frequently, and failure of the band brake and the friction material caused problems for him. We took brake bands off a new tractor to help him until a better brake design could be provided.

Shortly after the New Jersey trip, engineering was asked to send someone to see Oliver dealer Johnny Wheeler in Lubbock, Texas. His customers had several brake failures while operating on the level plateaus. We examined the failed brake parts and then went to see the customers. The farmers had recently learned that if they tilled in a contour pattern, rather than in a straight line, they could reduce or nearly prevent wind erosion. In order to steer the tractors on the contour surface with the wide imple-

ments they used, it was necessary to use the brakes heavily. The nearly constant braking required in these conditions caused the friction material and bands to fail frequently.

We brainstormed about this problem and agreed that we should set up a test to duplicate the field failures. We established a figure-eight test area on some concrete. The steering wheel was tied so that the steering could be done only by applying the brakes. The operator would travel 50 feet, steer to the right angle turn, travel 50 feet, and steer continuously on the figure-eight pattern. After approximately 30 minutes of the test, the binding material in the brake lining was failing. The brakes got very hot, and it did not take too long to duplicate what was happening in the field.

We decided that we must provide a brake that could dissipate heat as fast as it was generated and one where the temperature created under these conditions would not exceed the failure point of the brake lining. We invited brake companies to observe our tests and then provide us with some brakes to test. We tried some, and all showed some improvement over our production brakes, but none met our requirements.

We finally contacted Dent Parrott of Auto Specialties Company in St. Joseph, Michigan. He became very interested in our problem. We worked

with him on the application of a double-disc brake to our 88 tractor. The brake showed promise during the figure-eight test. We continued to test, evaluate, and improve until we came up with the brake that met our requirements. These tests occurred in 1949 and early 1950. We started producing double-disc brakes on the Fleetline tractors in late 1950 and early 1951.

Safety

Oliver developed guidelines concerning the best relationship between the operator and the tractor's controls, such as brake pedals, throttle, gearshifts and PTO controls. We created a one-half size plastic silhouette named "Oscar" that had ankles, knees, hips, wrists, elbows, and shoulders that pivoted. Oscar could be placed on the tractor seat of a half-size drawing to test the operator's relationship to the controls.

Electric Lights

My family bought a Farmall Regular tractor in 1927. We farmed more than 360 acres with this small tractor, horses, and mules. In 1928, my brother Lloyd and I equipped the tractor with electric lights so that we could operate it during the night. Using clamps, we mounted a generator from a 1924 Chevrolet on the right side, driven from the belt pulley shaft. Another set of clamps was made to mount the generator on the drawbar and drive it from the power take-off shaft when the tractor was used for belt work. We bolted angle irons to the left and right drive housings inside each rear wheel. We then used four Dodge headlights, two mounted to the angle irons facing forward, one on the right side facing rearward, and the fourth on the Farmall steering sector, which was located in the front, ahead and above the tractor radiator. This fourth headlight turned when the tractor was steered and lit the area where the tractor was turning.

We traded up to a Farmall F-30 for more power and transferred all of our lighting from the original Farmall, except the fourth light, which could not be used on the F-30 because of an enclosed worm pinion and sector.

Oliver first offered electric lights as an option on the Oliver 70 Row Crop tractors in 1935. The front lights were located on each side of the grille. A rear light to illuminate implements was located on the right rear wheel guard facing rearward. The Oliver 60 had forward and rearward lamps on the right wheel guard. One forward working lamp was mounted on the left wheel guard.

The Fleetline 66, 77, and 88 followed the Model 60 light locations. The advantage of these locations was that they provided more floodlighting on front-mounted working implements, such as cultivators.

One of the first problems of the test tractors during late 1944 and early 1945 near Phoenix, Arizona, was lighting failure after a short time of operation. The long staple cotton stalks tore the light wires from the tractor. The wires were installed between the main frame and the wheel guard, and the lights were located on some temporary wheel guards that were designed for older tractor models.

To solve this problem, I designed a wiring setup whereby the wires from the light switch were mounted on the inside of the operator platform flange to the rear-axle area. Then the wires passed through a steel tube attached to the rear side of the axle housing and the inside of the wheel guard. The light wires were then attached in a protected area of the wheel guard and extended to the lights mounted on the wheel guard. This improvised wiring pattern

was so successful that nighttime operation in the Phoenix area continued satisfactorily.

For the production models, grooves for the light wires and a recess for the cover plate were added to the rear side of the axle carrier's hexagon shape. The hexagon shape of the axle carrier was chosen by both the Oliver tractor and implement engineering departments. This shape became an accurate and solid mount for implements. The production light wires were mounted on the inside of the operator platform flange. A steel tube protected the wire to the recess in the axle carrier. The wire then passed through the recess, through the axle carrier flange, and then inside the wheel guard support channel to the light and light bracket.

The production light bracket was a steel stamping with strengthening ribs. It was attached to the wheel guard by bolts through the wheel guard and through the support channel. The result was a sturdy support for the light. Failure of the wheel guard on some competing tractors was a problem because the lamp bracket was attached to the wheel guard with insufficient support. As a result, the thin metal around the lamp and its bracket would crack. Such a failure did not occur on the Oliver Fleetline Tractors.

A common failure on earlier models was the cracking of the wheel guard around the lamp bracket. The Fleetline tractors were all released with an improved wheel guard and cast-iron lamp bracket that avoided this problem.

The Fleetline series of tractors had a number of features that reflected Oliver's commitment to operator comfort. One of the areas in great need of improvement was the seat. This photograph shows the old-style rigid, canvas-style seats, which were very uncomfortable for the operator.

One of the design criteria for the Fleetline tractors was to provide more comfort for the operator. This Ridemaster seat with rubber torsion support was designed to do just that and was very popular with the customers.

Ridemaster Seat

A main consideration in the development of the famous Fleetline 66, 77, and 88 tractors was to provide an easy-riding seat. Oliver conducted much research on the riding capabilities of seats in trucks, automobiles, and other vehicles. Bostrom Manufacturing Company in Milwaukee, Wisconsin, was a leader in the research for easier riding seats for trucks and off-road vehicles. This company had developed an in-depth research program to improve riding comfort. Bostrom became interested in Oliver's seat project and conducted studies on farm equipment.

Many designs were considered and some were tested in cooperation with Bostrom. One used a modified shock absorber, but it did not provide the desired smooth ride. The design chosen was a

seat mounted on torsional rubber springs. Much data was obtained on the movement of the vehicle versus the movement of the farmer. With this unit, there was little up and down movement of the farmer when the tractor ran over rough ground. Oliver's Ridemaster seat was introduced in 1949 on the Fleetline tractors.

The new seat suspension system was made by Bostrom, the supports were manufactured by Oliver, and the steel stamped pan and the cushion were purchased from other sources.

It was 1960 before John Deere introduced tractors with an easy-riding seat. Other companies also started providing an easy-riding seat on their tractors, but all much later than Oliver.

Outsourced Parts
Carburetors

Carburetors were purchased from Carter and Marvel Schebler. At the start of the Fleetline tractor development, air cleaners were purchased from Donaldson in the Twin Cities area of Minnesota, then Donaldson expanded its manufacturing facilities to Iowa. Bob Larson was the sales representative who worked closely with tractor manufacturers. There was never a dull moment when Bob was present. One of his favorite expressions was, "Call me S.O.B., Sweet Old Bob." Some of the first dry-type air cleaners were purchased from United Air Cleaner.

Mufflers

Oliver was the first to use aluminized steel mufflers. We received some complaints from dealers that the mufflers were wearing out too soon and this was a warranty item, so we looked for a longer lasting material. We consulted steel companies that were experimenting with aluminized steel. Nelson Muffler Company of Stoughton, Wisconsin, purchased aluminized steel and made mufflers for Oliver. Later, when the automobile industry started using aluminized steel mufflers, the supply of aluminized steel was greatly reduced. We were asked to accept a substitute. We argued, but did not win. We substituted regular steel painted with high-temperature silicone paint until aluminized steel was available in larger quantities. Donaldson also made mufflers and was the second source.

Oil Seals

Oil seals were not expensive by themselves, but if an oil seal failed, it could be costly. Chicago Rawhide Company was one of the most helpful and dependable suppliers of oil seals for Oliver tractors. Jack Eirk was the sales representative calling on Oliver. National Oil Seal Company was another source for good oil seals.

Radiators

Radiators were purchased from Young, Modine, and possibly other companies.

Tires

Tires were provided by Goodyear, Goodrich, and Firestone. The cost of tires was a major factor in the overall cost of a tractor. Goodrich had a unique policy in which the company assigned sales representatives to individual companies. Stan Murray had Oliver as his only account and was the sales representative to all of Oliver plants and sales branches. There were many sales representatives from Goodyear and Firestone during the development of the Fleetline tractors and in successive years.

Quality Hardware and Bearings

Hardware was important to the overall quality of a tractor. At one time Oliver purchased both non-hardened and hardened capscrews and bolts of the same size. A check on the assembly line showed that some soft capscrews were being used where hardened capscrews were specified and vice versa. This problem was solved when the Charles City plant decided to use only hardened hardware. This eliminated purchasing, storage, handling, and other costs of having extra parts in inventory, so it became economical to purchase only hardened hardware.

Bearings were purchased from various sources. Timken Bearing Company and Bower Roller Bearing Company were the sources for tapered roller bearings. Tapered roller bearings were used throughout the transmission, differential, and final drive. We had a long-term relationship with Timken.

Hyatt Bearing Company also had a tapered roller bearing except that the rollers were barrel shaped. The advantage claimed by Hyatt was that their bearings would accept more deflection of the shaft or axle on which the bearing was mounted.

Ball bearings to be used in PTO units were purchased from New Departure and Bearing Company of America. Straight roller bearings were purchased from Torrington Bearing Company and McGill. When I met Kip Recor after I had just completed the power take-off design in 1945, he was on his first trip as an engineering representative of Torrington. I needed a needle bearing for the output shaft to provide clearance for the clutch. Torrington was able to supply it, so Kip got his first bearing application. He was very happy. We became good friends.

Switches, steering wheels, wiring harnesses, gauges, lights, and a large number of items were also purchased.

Versatility

The versatility of the 66, 77, and 88, when designed together, created a custom-built combination. Many special assemblies of each model could be provided without designing many, if any, new parts.

The Oliver Fleetline tractors brought a host of improvements to the farmer, many of which were incorporated by competing manufacturers.

When Oliver put aluminized steel mufflers on the Fleetline tractors, it was the first time they were ever used. They were introduced to provide a longer-lasting muffler because mufflers were a warranty item that had to be replaced by dealers when they wore out too soon. The small aluminized mufflers on the Fleetline tractors were placed under the hoods.

The XO-121 Experimental Tractor

The XO-121 was a very important research program for Oliver. The engine used a raised compression ratio and specially developed fuel to dramatically improve on the power output and efficiency of comparable tractor engines. The research performed on this engine was used in the development of later Oliver production engines.

By 1953, the Ethyl Corporation became concerned about the success of the Oliver diesel tractors and their effect on the use and sale of tetra-ethyl lead for antiknock purposes in gasoline. If all agricultural tractors changed to diesel, the amount of tetraethyl lead sold would be greatly reduced.

Oliver was looking for improved tractor performance, especially lower fuel consumption with higher grade gasoline. So, Oliver and Ethyl developed a joint research program called the XO-121—"X" for experimental, "O" for Oliver, and "121" for a 12:1 compression ratio. There was a problem, however, because the Ethyl Corporation

board of directors did not want to approve the experimental program.

Charles F. Kettering of General Motors had directed the development of a high-compression automobile research engine that showed much promise in making gasoline engines more efficient. He was interested in the XO-121 project because he wanted to make gasoline engines that were more

fuel efficient than tractor diesel engines. Kettering finally convinced the Ethyl Corporation board of directors to approve the XO-121 project after Ethyl's laboratory management failed to sell the project to the board.

Executives of Ethyl and Oliver cooperated in the research program. Ethyl was to provide the experimental gasoline and monitor the design program at Charles City. Ethyl also agreed to conduct some engine tests in their laboratory in Detroit. Oliver's Charles City engineering department was responsible for the engine and tractor design and special parts. In fact, the project became so important to the two companies that the film, *Getting Ahead of Tomorrow*, was made about it.

An initial challenge was determining how much strength would be required in the crankcase assembly. We chose a four-cylinder Hercules diesel engine with multiple main bearings as a base for the engine design. We then proceeded with the design of the cylinder head, manifolds, carburetor, and other parts. A special tractor front frame was designed to accommodate the Hercules engine mounts and align the engine with the transmission input shaft. The radiator, air cleaner, sheet metal, and other parts were also Oliver's responsibility, as well as the assembly and field tests of the final tractor. Charles Van Over-

The research performed with the XO-121 was applied to later Oliver engines, especially the engine for the 1800, which used a raised compression ratio and concave piston crown to increase performance and efficiency. The Oliver Super series tractors also benefited from the XO-121 program research.

ABOVE: The 16mm film, *Getting Ahead of Tomorrow*, was about the development of the XO-121. This is a scene in the film where executives of Ethyl and Oliver discuss plans for the research tractor with a compression ratio of 12:1, which became the XO-121. Pictured, from left, are Rollin Gish, Richard Scales, George Bird, A. King McCord, Bynum Turner, Herb Morrell, and J. B. Macauley. Gish, Scales, Turner, and Macauley were with Ethyl Corporation and the others were with Oliver. *Author collection*

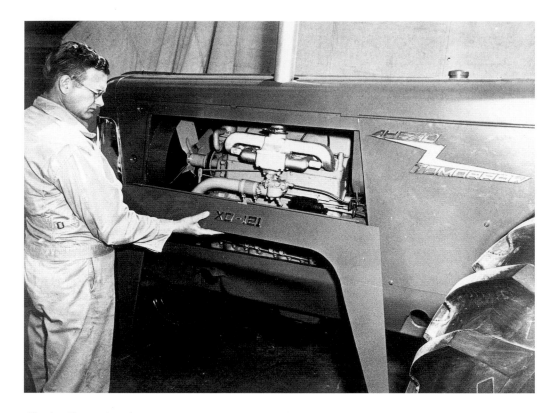

beke and Walter Roeming were the Oliver engineers responsible for the engine design. H. (Heine) Mueller and Keith L. (Punch) Pfundstein were the Ethyl Corporation's engineering representatives. Rollin Gish was in charge of the engine test program at the Ethyl Corporation's laboratory in Detroit, Michigan.

During May 1954 the XO-121 tractor was shipped to the General Motors proving grounds near Milford, Michigan, to be demonstrated for Ethyl and Oliver executives. Keith Pfundstein met Oliver's chairman, Alva Phelps, and president, A. King McCord, at the Detroit airport and drove them to the GM proving grounds. Phelps argued that the XO-121 was a waste of Oliver's resources and a waste of his time because it had no apparent purpose and so proved nothing. McCord tried his best to convince Phelps to be patient and open-minded. Both Phelps and Charles F. Kettering had come from General Motors, so McCord reminded Phelps what Kettering's high-compression Oldsmobile engine at 12:1 compression ratio had meant to the industry.

Charles City engineering was responsible for producing the experimental tractor. Max Denham of the Experimental Engineering Department is shown here with the XO- 121.

The XO-121 was tested by plowing a field with Max Denham of Oliver engineering as the driver. This and other tests in Charles City proved that the 12:1 compression ratio was practical, providing that gasoline of the required high quality became available. *Floyd County Historical Society*

When Phelps and McCord arrived at the proving grounds, Heine Mueller and Rollin Gish were plowing with the XO-121 tractor. McCord and Kettering drove the tractor with Rollin Gish riding along to answer any questions. When the tractor pulled up to the group, Kettering walked to it and gingerly touched the muffler, saying, "It can't be very hot because at 12:1, there can't be much heat left over."

The tractor performed exceptionally well. At the conclusion of the demonstration, Phelps was in favor of continuing the XO-121 program. After the demonstration, Keith Pfundstein drove Kettering to the airport. Kettering was quite talkative and friendly and apparently was pleased with what he observed at the demonstration. They were discussing research and applications of the new technology when Kettering uttered one of his famous expressions, "It's amazing what foolish thoughts I have when I think too long alone."

The program developed as planned and the results were beyond our expectations. The engine provided 43 percent more power with 28 percent less fuel. And the brake-specific fuel consumption of 0.385 pounds per horsepower-hour was equal to that of the best diesel engines.

During the 1954 American Society of Agricultural Engineers meeting at the University of Minnesota I presented a technical paper entitled, "Looking Ahead of Tomorrow in Tractor Engine Design," with Homer Dommel as co-author. There were many questions and good discussion. My friend Stanley Madill, a top engineering executive of Deere and Company, made an interesting comment to me afterward. He said, "You will never know what you have just done for John Deere engineering." His meaning became clear when John Deere introduced its new line of high-compression tractor models—the 1010, 2010, 3010, and 4010—in 1960 with vertical multiple-cylinder engines that made their old two-cylinder engines obsolete.

Oliver was host to a luncheon after the paper was presented. The guests included many media representatives, executives of the American tractor companies, and ASAE staff members. The luncheon

The XO-121 four-cylinder engine displaced 199 cubic inches, had a 3 3/4x4-inch bore and stroke, and overhead valves. The engine proved that higher compression ratios could, with high-quality fuel, produce more power and efficiency.

speaker was Charles F. Kettering of General Motors, who is considered the Thomas Edison of the automotive industry. He was the owner of approximately 200 patents, owned a large amount of GM stock, and was a major contributor to the Sloan-Kettering Cancer Research Center in New York City. He was in demand as a public speaker because he always held his audience spellbound.

Kettering told a story during the luncheon about his development of 10- and 12-inch-diameter pistons for the Electromotive Division of GM. During the development, he called a meeting and asked the engineers, "Why hasn't anyone made aluminum pistons for high-speed diesel engines?"

The answer was that aluminum was a softer metal than steel and would not withstand the high pressures of diesel combustion. He said that he was tired of his staff of young, bright engineers telling him that an aluminum piston that size cannot survive the high pressures and temperatures of a diesel engine. He told them that he did not want to hear

that again unless the engineer himself had firsthand experience as a piston inside a diesel engine. The aluminum would just need some reinforcing ribs, he suggested, and soon aluminum became the preferred material for high-speed diesel engine pistons.

During the luncheon he also related that he had recently attended a meeting with representatives from the American Petroleum Institute regarding the future for improved gasoline quality. He was told that the cost of high-quality gasoline would be prohibitive. He then asked, "If that is the case, maybe we are headed in the wrong direction. How about making 60 octane gasoline?"

He was told that the cost of producing 60 octane gasoline would also be prohibitive. Kettering then replied, "Then what in the hell is the relationship between octane rating and the cost of gasoline?"

Kettering was very interested in the XO-121 program and he was kept informed of its progress. During the luncheon meeting, he said, "I have made some evaluations and if all gasoline engines had this

LOOKING AHEAD OF TOMORROW IN TRACTOR ENGINE DESIGN

The following was presented at the national meeting of the ASAE at the University of Minnesota, Minneapolis, Minnesota on June 20-23, 1954 and was co-authored by T. H. Morrell, Chief Engineer, and H. K. Dommel, Supervisor of Experimental Engineering, both from the Oliver Corporation. The paper was reprinted with permission from ASAE.

The management at Oliver has always felt a keen sense of responsibility to our good dealers and their farmer customers. Part of this obligation is to keep ahead of tomorrow not only in tools and implements but also in the design of power plants.

We have continuously studied trends in connection with progress in agriculture and its mechanization. The economic factors that are so very important when it comes to designing, manufacturing, and marketing farm machinery have also been considered in our long-range planning activities.

An example of our interest and planning in connection with tractor power plants was the introduction of diesel engines for all models of our wheel tractor line and a short time later LP gas engines. These developments support a policy of investigating all the potentialities of the various engine types in order to provide the most efficient power plant regardless of fuel type. And to us, the best all-around tractor power plant is one that does the intended job most effectively and at the lowest cost to the individual customer.

In analyzing the trends in both quantity and quality of the various fuels available to farmers, it was noted that gasoline continues to be the most widely used fuel. In addition to its broad availability, the anti-knock quality of gasoline had been steadily increasing. For example, the octane number of regular gasoline, as determined by the Motor and Research Methods of testing, has increased from 75.5 and 80 in 1947 to 81 and 85.5 I 1954. These are the two accepted methods of determining the anti-knock quality of gasoline. In studying this quality trend we found that the average octane number of today's regular gasoline is higher than that of premium gasoline of 1947. It is generally accepted that this upward trend will continue.

Now—just what are the prospects of taking advantage of this gasoline quality trend by engine design? What does this octane number increase mean in terms of engine efficiency? These questions recall our experience back in the early 1930s when we capitalized on the improved regular gasoline octane number by introducing what was then a high compression tractor—the Oliver 70. We learned from this development that compression ratio was the principal key to transforming higher octane value into engine efficiency. This finding did not come easily. It required thorough study, not only of higher compression ratios but their proper integration with all of the engine design factors which are related to power and economy.

In studying the potentialities of projected fuel anti-knock quality, it was considered advisable to attempt to get ahead of tomorrow—to take a giant step forward. Such a step would require a comprehensive experimental program—a program to prove whether a tractor engine of advanced high compression design, using fuel "ahead of tomorrow," would really produce sound, practical, and realistic gains. We needed an experimental engine which could be used as a tool to accomplish this job.

To make this extension of our earlier study we called on the Ethyl Corporation. We felt that since they had been over similar ground before with automotive engines, their background would assist us in gaining the maximum potential benefits from high-compression design.

The decision to take a giant step forward was predicated on the possibilities of obtaining the objectives of efficient flexible power, economy, and long life by the application of high compression and structural rigidity.

In any type of exploratory research the engineer must sooner or later take a leap in the dark. Some progress can be made by inching cautiously forward, but advancing by small increments will not always pay off when you really want to push back the horizon of knowledge and gain a amount of radically new information. These principles of exploratory research certainly apply in the field of tractor engine design. Since the introduction of gasoline engines

This right-side view of the XO-121 engine shows most of the accessories, such as the alternator, distributor, and the ignition coil. The crankcase was taken from a four-cylinder Hercules diesel engine, while the top end of the engine was constructed by Oliver. The diesel crankcase and the XO-121 cylinder head made a good combination. Author collection

into the farm tractor field, compression ratios have in general moved upward to over 6 to 1. Even though the returns from a continued inching forward above 7 to 1 can be worthwhile, we felt that there was much more to be learned by making a real leap into the future.

With the decision approved to take this leap, it was necessary to decide how high in compression ratio we should go. While it was desirable to explore this variable as far into the future as possible, we knew of no such engine research efforts which went much beyond the level of 12 to 1. This compression ratio was selected since we felt that it was far enough ahead of present practice to yield a clear-cut answer to our major question: Will the high-compression route really yield major improvements in power and economy? The experimental fuel prepared for the compression ratio of 12 to 1 has basic characteristics similar to present day commercial gasolines, but has an anti-knock value beyond the conventional octane number scale. It is estimated that its equivalent octane number is approximately 101 Motor Method and 107 Research Method.

With the compression ratio of 12 to 1 selected, the necessary theoretical calculations of power output were made. We established the displacement of the engine so that its power output could be adequately handled by our 3-4 plow Model 88 tractor chassis which we feel is a very practical size tractor. On this basis, we would later be able to make some very fairly direct comparisons of results. For this engine we selected a diesel block with a displacement required to produce the power output desired and which had ample rigidity to provide a sufficient safety factor. A cylinder head was designed having a combustion chamber configuration which had demonstrated it was capable of utilizing high fuel anti-knock quality effectively. A conventional manifold and carburetor were used. A 12-volt ignition system was selected. It was designed to be functional and practical, and not a hot rod type of engine.

We would be presumptuous indeed at this point to say that our initial specifications for the engine represented the final word in design. In any exploratory design a certain number of compromises are forced on the engineer, and already many features have been tested and modified as necessary compromises were explored. Again, we would like to emphasize that the present design as agreed to, and the experimental engine as built does not repre-

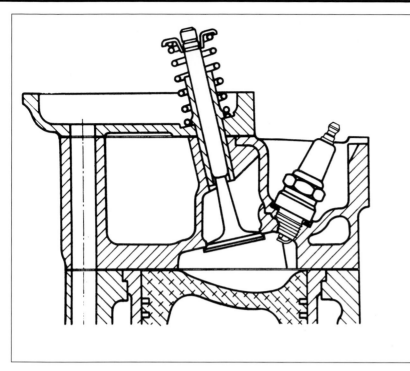

The most efficient combustion chamber shape for the XO-121 was a wedge-shaped cylinder head with a concave piston.

sent anything in the way of a frozen or finalized research tool. It is not, nor will it ever be, a production engine. It is a research tool to be worked with, to be studied, and it undoubtedly will be modified still further as our investigations continue. However, with its present specifications we believe it is one of the most useful, yes, one of the most startling tools ever developed in the long history of tractor power improvement.

We refer to the engine as the XO-121, the X for experimental, the O for Oliver, and the 121 denoting a 12 to 1 compression ratio. The XO-121 is a 199-cubic-inch overhead-valve, four-cylinder engine with a bore and stroke of 3-3/4 by 4-1/2 inches, and a governed speed of 1600 rpm.

The first dynamometer studies were directed toward finding out whether our earlier calculated enthusiasm could be justified. The criterion for this evaluation was primarily power output and fuel economy.

Results showed that our efforts had paid off. At best economy carburetor setting and all accessories, the engine developed 57.5 corrected brake horsepower at the flywheel with a fuel economy of .385 pounds per horsepower-hour. This was well within the range which had been predicted and, gentlemen, now to the best of our knowledge we had constructed the most efficient tractor engine ever built. Further checks indicated that friction, torque, and roughness were quite satisfactory. We, naturally, were interested in other yardsticks of performance such as volumetric efficiency, brake mean effective pressure, fuel distribution, and thermal efficiency. Checks of these items also supported the conclusion that the first progress report was an exceptionally good one.

To get an idea of the magnitude of the improvement shown in the XO-121, we made some comparisons at this point with the Model 70 engine of 1935 and with our present Model 77 (Table I). All three engines have substantially the same displacement and are governed at approximately the same speed. On the basis of horsepower output per cubic inch, we were 92 percent better than the 70 and 44 percent better than the Model 77. Looking at fuel economy, the gains were 36 percent and 30 percent respectively. There is no doubt about the value of the gains resulting from a well-designed, high-compression engine which takes full

advantage of gasoline anti-knock quality. Furthermore, it has been demonstrated that these gains can be realized without restoring to unconventional engine construction.

From this point on, our efforts were divided into two paths. It was desirable to install the experimental engine in a conventional tractor chassis for the purpose of belt and drawbar comparison tests, and at the same time we knew that further dynamometer studies and refinements were needed.

For several weeks belt and dynamometer tests were underway simultaneously, and we have to date approximately 1,100 hours of test experience with this design.

We also gained valuable experience with field drawbar work, such as the evaluation of rear wheel torque characteristics and the response of the engine to governor action and rate of load application. We wanted to be sure that such an engine would produce, not only on the dynamometer, but also under actual field conditions of variable speed and load at both part and full throttle.

When measured at the belt, the XO-121 was approximately 92 percent better than the 70 and 48 percent better than the 77. Looking at fuel economy, the gains were 40 percent and 32 percent. On the drawbar, the power of the XO-121 is approximately 85 percent and 43 percent better than the 70 and 77, respectively, and fuel economy is 35 percent and 28 percent improved. These results proved that the outstanding performance on the laboratory dynamometer were sound and could be realized in belt and drawbar work.

In attempting to appraise the value of our work to date, we recognize that we have really just completed the first step in a basic research program. We have looked ahead of tomorrow and we like what we see. Much work still remains to be done even before we can consider how improvements found might be passed on to the farmer in the future. However, we feel that our efforts have been well rewarded and that we have answers to the basic questions that were in our minds not so long ago. These answers are:

1. The principle of high compression as a means of gaining power and economy in farm tractor engines is practical and sound. Both theory and application have been confirmed by this experiment at a compression ratio of 12 to 1.

2. The level of improvements in power and economy at both full and part throttle are so attractive as to warrant further studies. These will include studies of compression ratios below 12 to 1 and their utilization of fuel anti-knock quality so that as improved fuel anti-knock quality is available, we will be in a position to take advantage of it. This, then, will narrow the gap between this basic research tool and current engines anfuels.

3. The performance of this engine in the tractor chassis demonstrated that as far as ease of starting, flexibility, and smoothness are concerned, there are no operational problems which limit the use of compression ratios up to 12 to 1. It should be repeated that this engine, which we call the XO-121, is a research tool, and is not an engine that will ever be in production.

TABLE I
Comparison of Performance of the XO-121 With Other Oliver Tractor Engines

Engine Dynamometer

MODELS	70	77	XO-121
Displacement, cubic inches	201	194	199
Compression Ratio	6.50:1	6.75:1	12:1
Governed Speed, rpm	1500	1600	1600
BHP-100 percent Maximum Corrected	31.6	41.22	60.9
BHP-Operating Maximum Observed	28.4	36.4	54.0
Horsepower-Hours Per Gallon, Operating Maximum	11.85	12.40	16.07

After the experiment was completed, the XO-121 tractor was given to Iowa State University, where it was displayed for many years. Later it was used at the Living History Farm outside Des Moines, Iowa. Finally it was acquired by the Floyd County Historical Society and is now at the group's museum in Charles City.

high-compression ratio and the gasoline quality to match, we could stack railroad tank cars full of gasoline from Chicago to New York and that would be our yearly saving of gasoline."

Research on gasoline engine efficiency continued, based upon what was learned from the XO-121. This information was very valuable to Oliver engineering at Charles City as a consideration for future tractor engine designs.

In September 1961, I presented the Society of Automotive Engineers technical paper, "Development of Oliver's New Gasoline Engine," at the Heavy Duty Vehicle Meeting held in Milwaukee, Wisconsin. Super 88 gasoline engines were modified and tested in many ways over several years. There were many things to consider, as described in the paper. Each item of change was studied and tested individually. Some of these tests required several hundred dynamometer hours.

Figure 13 of Appendix C shows the final combustion chamber configuration, which is a combination of the XO-121 and a concave piston head. This combustion chamber was introduced on the 1800 tractor in 1960. Nebraska test number 766 on the Model 1800 established a new all-time low fuel consumption record of 0.472 pounds per horsepower-hour or 13.18 horsepower per hour per gallon on the maximum power of the power take-off test. As far as we know, this record has not been broken at any official test laboratory. The paper indicates the in-depth study needed to design a tractor engine that would most efficiently utilize the quality of gasoline available when the 1800 tractor was introduced in 1960.

The XO-121 tractor was given to Iowa State University for display. The university kept it for many years and then gave it to the Living History Farms west of Des Moines. The tractor was repainted and almost lost its identity. The first president of the Hart-Parr/Oliver Collectors Association, Wayne Wiltse, was successful in getting the XO-121 tractor from the Living History Farms and brought to Charles City, where it was restored to its original colors. It is now a part of the Floyd County Museum in Charles City, Iowa.

After the introduction of the XO-121 tractor, Oliver sponsored a luncheon at the Curtis Hotel in Minneapolis for newspaper, radio, and television reporters and representatives of competitive tractor companies. Pictured, from left, are Herb Morrell, Charles F. Kettering of General Motors, and H. T. Mueller of Ethyl Corporation with the tractor. *Carl Rabe*

The XO-121 was used in the development of the Super Fleet of Oliver tractors, as can be seen in this promotional brochure, "Three Steps to Better Power."

The sensational XO-121 **. . . an experimental tractor**

News of a great new tractor with an amazing performance and economy record came out of Oliver's Charles City, Iowa, factory in the summer of 1954.

This exciting tractor—called the XO-121—delivered about 43 percent more power on 28 percent less fuel than tractors of the same size produced at that time.

But, since it had a compression ratio of 12 to 1, and required a specially blended fuel with an octane rating considerably above that generally used today, it was obviously far ahead of its time. Truly it was "ahead of tomorrow."

Although the XO-121 gasoline engine is the most efficient ever built, it cannot go into production. The XO-121 is purely an experimental

tractor. Nevertheless, as a research tool, it enabled Oliver engineers to evaluate how much power and economy could be obtained from higher compression and higher octane fuel. It answered important questions about the possibility of improving the performance and efficiency of present-day, mass-produced tractors.

Month by month, Oliver's far-sighted research program is accelerating the perfection of advancements for production line models. In fact, it has already resulted in the development of a completely new line of Oliver *Super* tractors.

Oliver is on a road clearly marked — better performance and greater economy from the high quality fuels now available.

Introduction of a New **OLIVER SUPER Fleet**

If there's a magic phrase that holds the secret of the greater and more efficient power of Oliver's new line of Super tractors, it is "high compression."

During the past few years the quality of gasoline has been vastly improved, and octane ratings have been climbing steadily. So, to realize more of the potential efficiency of today's fuel, Oliver designed engines to take advantage of it—based on the knowledge gained from operation of the experimental XO-121. Now, compression ratio has reached a new high for gasoline farm tractors — 7.0 to 1.

First of all, a higher compression ratio gives Oliver Super tractors far more horsepower than its predecessors. And, hand in hand with

more horsepower came another satisfying benefit, extremely important if you're contemplating the purchase of a new tractor. That benefit is *economy*—far greater economy. Oliver Super engines squeeze more work out of every drop of fuel.

Lastly, compression ratio has effected other changes in Oliver engine design. Super engines are more

ruggedly built, cylinder blocks and crankshafts are precision made to lower loss of power through friction. Carburetors and manifolds are constructed to permit the engine to "breathe" better.

Make your next tractor an Oliver Super—the tractor with the advantages of tomorrow's tractors—*today!*

THE SUPER TRACTORS

In the late 1940s, Ford Motor Company sold a large number of Model 8N tractors. Alva Phelps, Oliver's CEO, established a mandate for Oliver to copy the 8N tractor. The Ford-Ferguson 9N preceded the 8N and was introduced in 1939, but around 1947 Ford and Ferguson dissolved their partnership, and Ford continued with basically the same tractor called the Model 8N. Ferguson sued Ford for patent infringement and sought damages of about $340 million. During the early 1950s, this lawsuit was settled with Ford paying about $9 million to Ferguson. Those of us in Oliver's Charles City engineering department expected Ford to soon release a new, more modern tractor that would avoid infringing upon Ferguson patents, and we advised Oliver not to copy an old, obsolete tractor. But Oliver's Phelps would not change his mandate, because he thought Oliver could sell such a tractor in large quantities.

To avoid the Ferguson patents, Oliver engineering worked with Vickers to provide a draft control valve to be compatible with its continuous-running hydraulic pump. The rest of the tractor was basic and similar to the Ford 8N. We built a prototype to review with Alva Phelps and Oscar Eggen, vice president of engineering.

But we in Charles City were so certain that Ford would release a more modern tractor that we devoted more time to the Super 55 design with the independent power take-off, helical gear transmission, four-cylinder Super 66 engines, easy-riding seat, and many other innovations for a modern tractor.

Ford had a special sales show in Des Moines, Iowa, on November 30, 1953. Oliver's Des Moines sales branch had a combination Oliver/Ford dealer invite me to attend the show. At the show, Ford introduced the NAA "Jubilee" model. The Ford NAA had the advantages over the 8N that we had anticipated and were planning for in the Oliver Super 55.

On the following Monday, I participated in a conference call between Oscar Eggen and Alva Phelps of Oliver's Chicago office and George Bird, Charles City plant manager. They gave us approval to go ahead with the advanced Super 55 tractor design rather than our copy of the Ford 8N. Six Super 55 prototypes, known as XO-67s, were built in June of 1953. A pilot run of 300 Super 55 tractors was later requested by June 1954. The Super 55 was to be introduced with the new Super 66, 77, and 88 in late summer.

Our Charles City engineering department had always worked closely with the foundry, tool design, machine shop, and other depart-

The Fleetline tractors were upgraded in 1954 to the Supers, with open cowlings over the engines and a few upgrades. This is a diesel-engined high-crop version of the Super 88. The Super 88 was built from 1954 to 1958.

ABOVE: This X-67 tractor was the prototype Super 55. Six X-67s were produced in June 1953. This is one of them. *Carl Rabe*

This 1954 advertisement for the Super 55 touts Oliver's new model. This was an entirely new utility tractor designed for future needs, including operator comfort and safety, easy maneuverability, and high efficiency. *Floyd County Historical Society*

ments. We had embarked on crash programs before, but this one was more intense than others. We released the rear main frame drawings to start making production patterns even before we had assembled a prototype. We kept in touch with the foundry and requested that they tell us the cut-off date after which no more changes could be made.

There was much give and take among all departments. We shared the same goal of a pilot run of 300 in June 1954. We assembled four experimental models, one of which was to remain in Charles City, and three were sent to Bakersfield, California, for testing under the supervision of our field test engineer, Joe Roland. All of the reports were good.

We also conducted the usual accelerated tests on each component assembly, such as the hydraulic system, transmission, and power take-off. The purpose of these tests, which were performed in the Charles City experimental engineering department, was to prove the unit and compare the results with those from tests on assemblies with known components. We made the pilot run as scheduled and the tractors were distributed. Then, early production runs of 4,000 were scheduled to be manufactured in the fall of 1954. The first production run was completed and the tractors were shipped when a call came from Joe Roland that a fan on one of the Super 55 tractors had broken and gone through the radiator.

We quickly reviewed and tested the Charles City tractor with a high-speed camera and a strobe light. We learned that the fan blade tips were bending about 3/16 of an inch when they passed by the lower tank of the radiator. This deflection of the fan blade was enough to cause early failure. Generally, the fan blades do not pass by the upper or lower radiator tanks, but in order to have a low silhouette Super 55, this compro-

Oliver introduced the new Super 55 tractor in 1954. This Super 55 with a manure spreader demonstrates the high utility of this tractor. Its four-cylinder engine with aluminum pistons could attain speeds of 2,000 rpm.

A 1954 advertisement for the Super 55. *Floyd County Historical Society*

mise was necessary. We quickly set up a severe test and failed a fan in less than four hours of operation.

Meanwhile, we were in touch with suppliers to obtain a more sturdy fan that would not deflect and fail. We obtained some samples to test and found one that did not deflect and did not fail in our severe test. Our service department prepared a program to replace all Super 55 fans on the pilot and first production runs. I am not aware of any failure of the improved fan on any customer's tractor.

The Super 55 had helical gears in the first production assemblies. Because of the overlap of the gear teeth provided by the helical gears, the helical gear transmissions were very quiet.

The Super 55 became the 550 in 1958. It was considered a top performer in its field. Its stability, easy-riding seat, independent PTO, helical gear transmission, proven gasoline or diesel engine, and other advantages made it a formidable competitor. Oliver did not sell them in large enough quantities, however, to lower the cost of manufacture to a competitive per-unit cost. By this time, most other tractor companies also had comparable utility tractors. By the early 1960s, less expensive foreign tractors began to dominate the small agricultural tractor market in the United States. As coordinator of outside products

from 1965 to 1970, I worked with Fiat in Italy to purchase tractors for Oliver—the Model 1250, 1450, 1255, and 1355.

Super 66, 77, 88, and 99

In 1953, Oliver engineering at Charles City was asked to update the 66, 77, and 88 with more power and to introduce them as Super models. So, in addition to the crash program on the Super 55, we also had to provide pilot runs of 300 each of the Super 66, 77, and 88 for introduction in late summer. At the same time, we were preparing the paper on the XO-121 for the American Society of Agricultural Engineers summer meeting at the University of Minnesota in June 1954, and we were beginning the preliminary specifications for the experimental 1800 and 1900 tractors to be introduced in 1960. We were very busy.

The Super 66, 77, and 88 styling remained basically the same as the 66, 77, and 88, except the side panels to the engine compartment were opened to provide better movement of air and engine cooling.

The four-cylinder 66 engine was changed from a bore of 3 5/16 inches to 3 1/2 inches, and the speed was increased from 1,600 to 2,000 rpm. The higher speed required counterbalancing the crankshaft and changing from cast-iron to aluminum pis-

The Oliver Super 66 tractor used the Model 66 chassis with the Super 55 2,000 rpm engine with aluminum pistons. This is a 1954 Super 66 diesel tractor with a single front wheel.

This diesel-engined 1955 Super 66 is equipped with the adjustable front axle.

tons. Both the gasoline and diesel 66 engines were also used in the Super 55. The six-cylinder 77 engines were changed from a bore of 3 5/16 inches to 3 1/2 inches, but the speed remained at 1,600 rpm. The 88 engines were changed from a bore of 3 1/2 inches to 3 3/4 inches with the speed remaining at 1,600 rpm.

A pilot run of 300 each of the Super 66, 77, and 88 tractors was produced for introduction during the summer of 1954. Production runs of the Super models followed in the fall of 1954. The Super models continued in production through part of 1958.

The Super 99 was designed and built by Oliver's South Bend tractor plant. It had the basic chassis of the 99. The engine was the General Motors two-cycle 371 diesel, which had three cylinders with 71 cubic inches of displacement per cylinder. The Super 99 was also available with an Oliver six-cylinder gas or diesel engine having a 4-inch bore and 4-inch stroke. The different engine required a new front frame, but the styling was the same as the other Super models.

A 1955 Super 66 with wide front end and diesel power. A Super 66 Diesel tested at Nebraska in 1955 produced 22.49 drawbar and 33.69 belt horsepower.

A 1958 Super 66 with single front wheel. A Super 66 burning gasoline tested at Nebraska in 1955 put out 22.36 drawbar and 32.83 belt horsepower.

In the Super 77 tractors increased power was obtained from these six-cylinder engines by increasing the bore size from 3 5/16 inches to 3 1/2 inches while using aluminum pistons and 1,600 rpm maximum speed. This is a 1955 Super 77 standard tread model.

Model 550, 660, 770, and 880

In 1957, Oliver engineering at Charles City was asked to upgrade the Super models to provide more power. The 550 and 660 engines had a bore increase from 3 1/2 inches to 3 5/8 inches, and the speed remained at 2,000 rpm. The 550 continued in production from 1958 to 1975. The 660 continued in production from 1959 to 1964.

The 770 tractor engines were increased in speed from 1,600 to 1,750 rpm. Many other changes were made at this time, such as the crankshaft, alu-

minum pistons, and gasoline combustion chamber. The 770 continued in production from 1958 to 1967.

The 880 tractor engines had a speed increase from 1,600 to 1,750 rpm. The bore and stroke remained the same as the Super 88. Other changes to the engines paralleled the 770. Early production 880 and all 770 tractors had spur gear transmissions. Later 880 tractors had the helical gears, making these transmissions quiet. The 880 tractor continued in production from 1958 to 1963, when it was superseded by the 1600 model.

In 1956 Oliver hired an industrial designer, Wally Droegemueller. He was very helpful in the styling of the 550, 660, 770, and 880 and other tractor models and products in other Oliver plants. Wally continued his work through the styling of the White tractors.

Power Booster Drive

The Power Booster Drive was introduced as an option for the 770–880 models. It had gears, a housing, and an over-running clutch. The regular gears were direct drive to the transmission. When the direct drive was released, the over-running clutch had pawls that would grip a slower shaft and cause a slower speed of the tractor. The result was about a 15 percent reduction in speed with approximately 15 percent extra pulling power. IHC was the first with this type of system, which they called Torque Amplifier. Our goal was to provide a simple mechanism and reduce the need for power shift transmissions. Our Charles City engineering department continued to search for the ideal power shift transmission.

Carl Hecker, president of Oliver at that time, requested that an experimental test be conducted with a General Motors four-cylinder diesel engine and a Hydramatic four-speed industrial power shift transmission. This combination was assembled in a Super 88 chassis. Oliver engineers were concerned about such a combination because of the cost and safety. The test was conducted in a field being plowed to plant corn. The field had a 30-foot-wide waterway in the middle of it. Our test driver was informed about what might happen when he actuated the Hydramatic system to raise the plow out of the ground. The test revealed what we had anticipated. When the plow came out of the ground, the Hydramatic power shift transmission shifted quickly through its four speeds and the tractor front wheels were raised about 4 feet off the ground. Consequently, our power shift transmission research continued.

The Super 88 tractor design increased power output by increasing the bore size from 3 1/2 inches to 3 3/4 inches with the same cast-iron pistons and a maximum engine speed of 1,600 rpm. This is a 1955 Super 88 Diesel Row Crop with extra high clearance.

A diesel-engined high-crop 1955 Super 88. An Super 88 Diesel tested at Nebraska in 1954 produced 37.93 drawbar and 47.7 belt horsepower.

The Power Booster Drive tests were completed in the laboratory and in the field with no problem. It was released for production. About this time, our suggestion committee decided to accept a suggestion to discontinue the transmission flushing operation on the assembly line. The flushing operation consisted of filling the transmission with oil, rotating the gears, and then draining the oil. The oil was then filtered and placed in a reservoir to be reused. Without the flushing operation, sand, shop dirt, and other dirt from handling and machining would remain in the transmission.

This 1956 photograph shows the Charles City plant's inventory of recently built Super tractors ready for customers. *Harold W. Snyder*

UPPER RIGHT: This billboard greeted Charles City, Iowa, visitors in 1956. *Harold W. Snyder*

The Oliver Model Super 99 tractor was an updated version of the 99 offered with an Oliver six-cylinder gas or diesel engine or a 371 GM Detroit diesel. This gasoline version was built in 1955.

The Power Booster Drive received its lubricants from a system circulating through the transmission. The over-running clutch acted as a centrifuge to collect and retain all of the contaminate particles. Without the flushing operation, these particles quickly built up and caused the surfaces of the over-running clutch pawls to wear. A worn over-running clutch could not grip the shaft, so it became nonfunctional.

The plant suggestion committee generally consisted of a representative from each major department, but the engineering representative was not present when the decision was made to discontinue the flushing operation. The net savings on the assembly line of discontinuing the flushing operation was less than $2 per transmission. But the cost to clean up all of the tractors and replace the over-running clutch and other worn parts on tractors that had been assembled and shipped cost millions of dollars. Guess who got blamed for the problem? Engineering. After this problem, all transmissions were turned upside down, and about 40 streams of oil under pressure washed out the transmission just before the transmission openings were covered. A special lubricating system with a filter was also included for the tractors having the Power Booster Drive.

Model 950, 990, and 995

The 950, 990, and 995 were South Bend tractor plant products that were moved to Charles City in 1958. The 950 had a six-cylinder Oliver diesel or gasoline engine with a bore and stroke of 4x4 inches. The displacement was 302 cubic inches, and the speed was 1,800 rpm. This tractor replaced the Super 99 six-cylinder series.

The 990 had the GM 371 diesel engine and was basically the same as the Super 99 with the GM engine. The engine speed was 2,000 rpm. The 995 used the same GM engine as the 990 but was equipped with an Allison Torque Convertor.

One-row Offset Tractors
Super 44

Oliver had several programs to develop a one-row offset tractor to compete with the Farmall Model A, which was introduced by the International Harvester Company in 1939. The small size of the little Farmall made it popular with small-acreage farms,

---

ENGINE *Make* Oliver *Type* 6 cylinder vertical *Serial No.* 949637 *Crankshaft mounted* lengthwise *Head* 1 *Lubrication* pressure *Bore and Stroke* 3¾" x 4" *Rated rpm* 1600 *Compression ratio* 7.00 to 1 *Displacement* 265 cu. in. *Port Diameter Valves Inlet* 1⅜" *Exhaust* 1¼" *Governor* variable speed centrifugal *Carburetor Size* 1" *Ignition System* battery *Starting System* 6 volt battery *Air Cleaner* oil washed wire mesh *Muffler* was used *Oil Filter* replaceable waste packed cartridge *Cooling medium temperature control* thermostat.

REPAIRS AND ADJUSTMENTS No repairs or adjustments.

REMARKS All test results were determined from observed data and without allowances, additions or deductions. Tests B and F were made with carburetor set for 100% maximum belt horsepower and data from these tests were used in determining the horsepower to be developed in tests D and H, respectively. Tests C, D, E, G, H, J and K were made with an operating setting of the carburetor (selected by the manufacturer) of 94.8% of maximum belt horsepower.

HORSEPOWER SUMMARY

	Drawbar	Belt
1. Sea level (calculated) maximum horsepower (based on 60° F and 29.92" HG)	49.81	58.08
2. Observed maximum horsepower (tests F and B)	47.08	55.77
3. Seventy-five per cent of calculated maximum drawbar horsepower and eighty-five per cent of calculated maximum belt horsepower (formerly ASAE and SAE ratings)	37.36	49.37

We, the undersigned, certify that this is a true and correct report of official tractor test No. 525.
L. F. Larson
Engineer-in-Charge
C. W. Smith (Chairman)
L. W. Hurlbut
F. D. Yung
Board of Tractor Test Engineers

The OLIVER Corporation, 400 West Madison Street, Chicago 6, Illinois   "Finest in Farm Machinery"

Three steps to better power

1 An experimental tractor

2 A new super fleet

3 A new economy record

by the OLIVER Corporation
Founders of the Tractor Industry

New OLIVER SUPER 88 with 7 to 1 compression ratio Gasoline Powered Model Sets Fuel Economy Record

Proof that Oliver's high-compression gasoline engines are the *economy* leaders is found in the Nebraska Test record of the new, 4-plow Super 88.

In this nationally recognized test, the Super 88 set a new economy record of .484 pounds of fuel per horsepower-hour.

"Pounds of fuel per horsepower-hour" is the measure of economy commonly used by tractor engineers. It is the number of pounds of fuel required to develop one horsepower for one hour.

You buy fuel by the gallon. But an engine burns it by the pound. You see, different fuels vary in weight per gallon, and even gasoline varies from one season to another in pounds per gallon. These variations do not affect the pounds per horsepower-hour fuel economy records.

The new Super 88 turned in another exceptional record in the Nebraska Test—6354 pounds of drawbar pull. In addition, it developed 58.08 maximum horsepower on the belt.

So, here is another result of Oliver's 7.0 to 1 compression ratio—*more power*—increased power that puts each Oliver Super in a higher power class.

See your Oliver dealer and get the full story on the *new, powerful, economical, modern* tractor fleet!

Reproduction in full of the OLIVER SUPER 88 Nebraska tractor test

NEBRASKA TRACTOR TEST No. 525
OLIVER SUPER 88 HC

Department of Agricultural Engineering, Univ. of Neb.
Dates of test: September 27 to October 16, 1954
Manufacturer: THE OLIVER CORPORATION, Charles City, Iowa
Manufacturer's rating: Not rated

BELT HORSEPOWER TESTS	Hp.	Crank shaft speed rpm	Fuel Consumption Gal. per hr.	Hp. hr. per gal.	Lb. per hp. hr.	Water used Gal. per hr.	Temp. deg. F. Cooling med.	Air	Barometer inches of Mercury
TEST B — 100% MAXIMUM LOAD — TWO HOURS									
	55.77	1601	4.509	12.37	0.496	0.00	179	68	28.950
TEST C — OPERATING MAXIMUM LOAD — ONE HOUR									
	53.14	1599	4.194	12.67	0.484	0.00	175	63	28.950
TEST D — RATED LOAD — ONE HOUR									
	49.59	1601	4.051	12.24	0.501	0.00	174	65	28.940
TEST E — VARYING LOAD — TWO HOURS (20 minute runs; last line average)									
	49.41	1597	4.048	12.21	0.503		174	60	
	1.94	1730	1.599	1.21	5.057		164	66	
	26.02	1678	2.884	9.02	0.680		167	66	
	51.28	1527	4.043	12.68	0.484		176	65	
	13.16	1694	2.185	6.02	1.019		165	65	
	37.96	1636	3.520	10.78	0.569		170	64	
	29.96	1643	3.046	9.84	0.624		169	64	28.930

TORQUE (At Dynamometer)

ENG. RPM	1595	1490	1397	1289	1199	1096	999	888	805	699
LB. FT.	332.7	340.7	343.9	344.2	346.0	347.7	347.7	346.3	346.3	345.6
DYN. RPM	831	777	727	672	625	570	520	461	418	362

A 1955 Super 99 diesel tractor The three-cylinder two-cycle GM engines on these tractors were equipped with superchargers.

This is a Super 99 gasoline tractor. The gas models were not equipped with the supercharger.

while the offset design made it an outstanding cultivating tractor. Specific aspects of the Model A's offset design were patented, which made it difficult for other companies trying to provide a comparable tractor.

Some Oliver executives suggested that Oliver make a tractor with the transmission on the right side by the right rear wheel and angle the engine and driveline toward the left front. A one-row cultivator could be mounted in the center of the tractor's rear end. Several evaluations were conducted on the feasibility of such a tractor, but feedback from the engineers was mostly negative. The executives proposing the design did not understand the feedback, however, and persisted in their request for such a design.

Oliver engineering at Charles City purchased an engine, transmission, and other assemblies to build one prototype tractor. The frame of the tractor was designed to fit these purchased items. The prototype tractor was referred to as "a tractor built to prove that a tractor shouldn't be built that way."

When I started to work for Oliver on October 4, 1944, the supervisor of experimental engineering, Tommy Martin, had a small farm a few miles south of Charles City. There, his close friends and

members of the Oliver engineering department had victory gardens (home gardens planted to increase food production during wartime). This tractor was available to all gardeners to use to cultivate the gardens, providing they were planted in 40-inch rows. The operator of this tractor could do well for a short time while cultivating, but soon became disoriented, watching the plants pass through a small opening behind the angled driveline and at the rear of the tractor. When cultivating, one also needs to look up at the row for some distance ahead, but obstructions to this line of sight made it hard for the operator to keep the cultivator accurately on the row of plants.

One of my assignments in the late 1940s was to administer the one-row offset tractor design. The design I recommended had the engine and transmission on the left side of the tractor. A prototype was built for viewing by some Oliver executives including Alva Phelps, the Oliver CEO, and Oscar Eggen, the vice president of engineering. We worked late two nights before their visit, but there were a few finishing touches left to do the morning before the viewing. A starter for the tractor had been selected and installed,

The Oliver Model Super 44 was designed as a one-row offset tractor for garden use or one-row crops such as tobacco. In fact, most of these tractors sold in the Carolinas and Virginia to cultivate tobacco.

Initially, a Cessna Hydraulic hydraulic system (which Minneapolis-Moline also used) was adapted to the Super 44. Problems developed with the system, so the hydraulic system from the Oliver 550 was adapted for the Super 44's replacement, the Model 440. The rear end is shown here with the hitch, PTO, and belt pulley.

but none of us had checked the direction of rotation needed for our tractor's special starter mounting. During the viewing, the starter turned the engine backwards, forcing us to hand crank it. This was one of my most embarrassing moments.

We operated this tractor at the plant and in the field. Then, it was decided to build four more prototypes—known as Model G experimentals—and send them to garden country for tests. These four units were loaned to a large farmer in the Rio Grande Valley in south Texas where we could get some 24 hours of operation per day. Herb Pyle was sent with the

units to monitor their operation and send us his weekly report on each tractor.

We thought that we had designed a foolproof transmission interlock mechanism to prevent the transmission from getting locked into two gears at once but, as in the original Fleetline testing, the operators managed to do it. Herb Pyle figured out how it could be done. The gearshift lever had to be pulled upward against the centering springs so that the end of the lever could pass over the notch in one transmission shifter rod while the tractor was in one gear. The gearshift lever then could engage the notch

The Super 44 was built in 1957 and 1958.

This photograph of an Oliver facility was taken in 1956. *Harold W. Snyder*

in another shifter rod. When the second shifter rod was moved to engage the gears for a new speed, the transmission locked in the two gears. The transmission cover would then have to be removed and both shifter rods returned to their neutral position before the tractor could continue in operation.

In the case of the Model G, the solution to the problem was different than in the 66, 77, and 88. We made some new transmission cover castings, machining the centering springs shallower and increasing their size. We sent them to Herb, who changed them in the tractors. They had no more problems with the transmissions getting locked in two gears.

A market survey was taken to determine the number of Super 44 tractors the Oliver tractor dealers could sell. As the result of the survey, the project was again deferred for more study and consideration.

Model 440

In 1953, the Charles City engineering department was asked to consider the possibility of building a tractor to compete with the IHC Super AV tractor. The Super AV had higher crop clearance for cultivating tall crops, such as asparagus and other raised-bed crops. We modified the 66 in an attempt to provide a suitable tractor, making 250 to 500 tractors per year without the high cost of special tooling and small production runs.

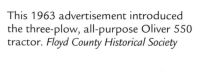

This 1963 advertisement introduced the three-plow, all-purpose Oliver 550 tractor. *Floyd County Historical Society*

The Model 550 and 660 tractors provided more power than the previous Super 55 and Super 66. This was accomplished by increasing the bore of the four-cylinder engine from 3 1/2 to 3 5/8 inches while retaining the same maximum speed of 2,000 rpm. This is a 1961 Model 660 with an adjustable wide front axle.

The modified 66 tractor had a single-row cultivator mounted on the right side, 42-inch rear tires, increased front axle height, and other changes. One unit was assembled with a mechanical power lift. One concern we had was whether the side draft cultivating only one row would be satisfactory. Our tests at Charles City were satisfactory, but the list price of this combination was approximately $150, or about 10 percent more than the IHC Super AV, so the proposal was tabled. Besides, the 66 itself had the power and flexibility to provide for two-row application.

In late 1953 or 1954, Oliver's Battle Creek aviation plant was in the process of discontinuing its work on the Boeing Aircraft Company's reconnaissance plane fuselages, so Oliver was looking for products to continue plant operation. The Charles City engineering department was asked to revive the one-row offset tractor designs and send all drawings and information to the Battle Creek plant. Charles City engineering recommended using the new Cessna Hydraulic hydraulic system (which Minneapolis-Moline was also using at the time) or the Super 55 hydraulics, if they could be developed quickly enough.

In the Oliver Model 770 tractors the six-cylinder engines used aluminum pistons and the required crankcase counterbalancing to allow for higher maximum engine speed of 1,750 rpm. This is a 1966 Model 770 with adjustable wide front axle.

OPPOSITE: The Model 660 was built from 1959 to 1964 and were available with gasoline or diesel engines. This is a 1961 Model 660.

A 1966 Model 770 wide front. An Oliver 770 tested at Nebraska in 1958 produced 34.92 drawbar and 48.8 belt horsepower.

The one-row offset tractor project did not stay at Battle Creek long. It was transferred to Oliver's South Bend tractor plant. Their engineering department adapted the Cessna hydraulic system and released the tractor Model Super 44 in 1957. When the South Bend tractor plant was closed in 1958, all tractor models were transferred to Charles City.

The Charles City service department soon learned that there were problems with the Cessna hydraulic system. This hydraulic unit had many adjustment provisions, which resulted in looseness between a large number of the control parts. The looseness in the control parts caused some erratic functioning of working equipment, such as a three-point hitch-mounted plow. We retained the most sensitive adjustment and then redesigned it to eliminate approximately 125 parts. We also attached the hydraulic unit more securely to the tractor. The Charles City engineering department then proceeded to adapt the 550 hydraulic system to the one-row offset tractor, which became the Model 440 in 1959 or early 1960. Sales of the Model 440 were low. Further consideration of adapting the modified 550 hydraulic system to the 440 was discontinued because the cost of the casting equipment and the tooling could not be justified economically.

A major change in the styling of Oliver tractors occurred with the introduction of the 550, 770, and 880 models. The new styling on this 1960 Model 880 standard tractor in the foreground contrasts with the older styling of the 1955 Super 55 in the background.

The Oliver Model 950 tractor had a 302-cubic-inch engine with the bore size and stroke both 4 inches and a maximum speed of 1,800 rpm. This one is a 1961 Oliver 950 standard tread tractor that burns gasoline.

Walt Roeming and Herb Morrell discuss the new 880 engine which included aluminum pistons and crankcase counterbalancing to allow for greater engine speeds. *Author collection*

This Model 880 had wheatland fender/cover guards. An Oliver 880 burning gasoline was tested at Nebraska in 1958 and produced 42.89 drawbar and 57.43 belt horsepower.

This shows a power hitch on a Model 880. An Oliver 880 Diesel tested at Nebraska in 1958 put out 41.74 drawbar and 59.48 belt horsepower.

A 1961 Oliver 950 standard tread tractor. An Oliver 950 Diesel tested at Nebraska in 1958 produced 48.76 drawbar and 67.23 belt horsepower.

The Oliver Model 990 tractor had the same General Motors engine as the Super 99, the GM-371. This example is a 1957 Oliver 990 Industrial.

The Oliver 950 was equipped with an Oliver 302-cubic-inch four-cylinder engine. This is a 1961 Oliver 950 standard tread tractor.

An Oliver 990 Industrial tested at Nebraska in 1958 produced 61.46 drawbar and 75.46 belt/PTO horsepower.

The Model 440 tractor was an updated version of the Super 44. This is a 1960 Model 440.

The Oliver 995 GM Lugmatic Torque Converter was called the "New Power Sensation in Farming" in this 1958 advertisement. *Floyd County Historical Society*

The Model 440 was an upgraded versions of the Super 44. This is a 1960 Model 440.

The Model 440 was built in 1960 and 1962.

ANOTHER NEW LINE

During the early 1950s the Charles City engineering department's research for the XO-121 and our experience with the Super models revealed some interesting economic issues. The main economic issues facing farmers were the increased cost of having an extra hired hand, the availability of hired hands, and the decline in the number of farmers. When we plotted these trends, it became obvious that by 1960 farmers would need extra power to farm the land that previously was farmed with the help of hired workers.

The 1800 was designed to be the Row Crop tractor to replace the hired hand. The 1900 was designed to be the larger Wheatland tractor. The 1600 and 1750 were smaller versions of the 1800 and were designed to be released later. The 1800 was used for most of the field and laboratory tests. The driveline of the 1900 was designed to meet the power requirements of more than 100 PTO horsepower.

Design criteria established for the larger Row Crop tractors included the innovations of the Fleetline 66, 77, and 88 but with increased power requirements, extra fuel capacity, and draft control. Four-wheel drive, with the front tires smaller than the rear tires, was also included as a design criterion.

Draft Control

Draft control is a function of the hydraulic system and the tractor hitch to the implement. When extra pulling power (draft) is required, the hydraulic system is actuated and it lifts the implement a slight amount to reduce the required draft. The implement then lowers itself to the preset position when there is less draft required.

The smaller tractors had a three-point hitch with the upper link containing the draft control sensing device. The two-plow implement on the small tractors was ideal for the upper link sensing device, but when a third bottom is added, it tends to stabilize the front bottom, causing the upper link sensing to the hydraulic system to be less effective. Four or more plow bottoms will cause the front bottom to be ineffective for good draft control. A study of the overall draft control system led to consideration of a two-point hitch with semi-mounted implements and draft sensing from the two lower links.

The South Bend engineering department was not enthusiastic about this new system and questioned if enough sensing from the lower links could be obtained. Charles City

This is a 1963 Model 1600. Equipped with a six-cylinder engine—either a 231-cubic-inch gasoline or a 265-cubic inch diesel—the Model 1600 was built from 1962 to 1964.

ABOVE: Walt Gardner drove the new 1800 into the Hippodrome arena with a mounted cultivator for its first introduction to the assembled dealers. The larger tractors, such as the 1800 and 1900, were designed for use with four or more plow blades. This created a need for stronger hitches and a different draft control system, so Oliver developed the two-point hitch with draft sensing from the lower links. *Chuck Dillman*

Both the 1800 and 1900 tractors were available with Terra tires. These large, low-pressure tires distributed the tractor's weight over a larger area and, therefore, decreased the weight per square inch tremendously. These tractors could be used where tractor tracks were undesirable, such as in sod production.

engineering conducted numerous mathematical calculations and converted a four-bottom pull-plow used in conjunction with an 1800 tractor. The furrow wheel was maintained as a means of having the two-link lower sensitivity. The first tests of the combined tractor and implement worked well but needed some refinements. Oliver provided the two links with a mechanism to permit the operator to stay on the tractor seat while hooking up an implement designed for the new lower links.

Independent Power Take-Off

The independent power take-off on the 1800 and 1900 had an oil clutch with hydraulic engagement inside the final drive area. There were several reasons for this location. First, the PTO had to be within the standards and there was not enough room for the clutch and the mechanisms at the rear of the tractor. Also, the PTO clutch would have been too difficult to operate manually from the operator's seat.

Engines

The 1800 engine was a revised 880 engine with larger cylinders that could attain higher speeds. The 1900 engine was a two-cycle, four-cylinder General Motors engine with 54 cubic inches of displacement in each cylinder. This GM 454 diesel engine was a relatively new design.

Cast-iron Grille

Oliver's design criteria included the provision that one-third of the weight of the basic tractor rest on the front wheels and two-thirds of the weight rest on the rear wheels. This required adding weight to the front of the front frame, so we added a heavy cast-iron grille to the 1800 and 1900 tractors. This added weight was necessary to provide stability when implements were added to equip the tractors for field use and was crucial to the overall stability of the 1800 and 1900 tractors.

Steering

These larger tractors were difficult to steer manually. First, the universal joint angles exceeded their angle capacity. Second, without some assistance, steering in most conditions required too much effort.

The Char-Lynn Company had just developed a hydrostatic steering mechanism, which permitted us to provide a tilt and telescoping steering wheel. With the tilt and telescoping steering wheel, the operator could stand up to rest from sitting and adjust the steering wheel to a comfortable position. In 1970, at the Farm Progress Show in Iowa, J. I. Case had an area for demonstrations and a program showing what was new on their tractors and equipment. One item on the program highlighted the "new" tilt and telescoping steering wheel. One

bystander said to another bystander, "Oliver has had the tilt and telescoping steering wheel for about 10 years, haven't they?"

Fuel Capacity

Oliver engineers listened to comments from everyone during the development of these new tractors, and having enough fuel capacity for an eight-hour day was a prime concern. Oliver developed additional fuel capacity by designing supplementary wheel guard fuel tanks. This made space a concern during the entire design effort. A familiar saying among the engineers was, "Let me hang the fuel tank and the battery compartment on a sky-hook, and then I will have enough room for everything else."

Gasoline and diesel versions of the Model 1600, both equipped with Hydra-Power, were tested at Nebraska in 1963. The diesel-engined tractor produced 57.95 PTO and 46.9 horsepower. The gasoline tractor put out 56.5 PTO and 47.09 drawbar horsepower.

Four-Wheel Drive with Terra Tires

The 1800 and 1900 four-wheel-drive tractors became a natural for the Terra tires made by Goodyear. The Terra tires required very low pressure and the ground area covered by them was much larger than with regular tractor tires, which made the Terra tires suitable for special applications. At one of the Farm Progress Shows in Iowa, Oliver representatives, guided by Dutch Zandbergen, conducted a remarkable demonstration of the Terra tires. They pressed chicken eggs, with the small ends down, into

the wet ground and then drove over them with the Terra tire-equipped tractor. The eggs did not break. The low ground pressure was advantageous when the tractors were used in fields growing sod and other crops, requiring that no tracks be left.

To research the applications most suited for Terra tires, I arranged to get a loan of a 1900 with Terra tires to be used for a short time in the sugar cane fields south of Lake Okeechobee, Florida, where crawler tractors were being used. This arrangement was made possible by Aubry Hedrick, the manager of the Atlanta,

In order to meet the anticipated future needs of farmers, the Oliver 1800/1900 series of tractors were designed for increased power, increased fuel capacity, and draft control. The 1800 and 1900 were very popular. The 1800 and 1900 were produced from 1960 to 1964 when they were replaced with the 1850 and 1950. This shows an Oliver 1800 doing the spring plowing. *J.C. Allen & Son*

In 1960, Oliver had been building six-cylinder tractors for 25 years. The 1935 Model 70, the first six-cylinder tractor, is shown with the 1960 Oliver 1800 and Charles City plant personnel (left to right) Bob Burgraff, Walt Gardner, Bill Sheeley, Jim Light, Herb Morrell, John Dorwin, Gene Brunsman, Jr., Merle Hicks, and George Bird. *Carl Rabe*

Georgia, sales branch. A few weeks later, I contacted Aubry to find out how the unit was performing. His reply was that he had sold it to a sod grower, a minor potential use of this special tractor. So much for my attempt to assist the Oliver sales department.

Safety Standards

Oliver emphasized safety considerations in the design criteria for the 1800 and 1900 tractors. The driver was to enter from the left side instead of the rear. The axle carriers were to be designed with enough strength to avoid failure when a fully equipped tractor was subjected to a rollover accident equivalent to twice the force of gravity. Oliver engineering became interested in Rollover Protective Structures (ROPS) as a result of accident reports and a 1953 Swedish technical paper on that subject, so ROPS were included in the design criteria.

When the 1800 and 1900 tractors were introduced in 1960, ROPS air-conditioned cabs and ROPS canopies were presented for production. A market survey by the Oliver sales department indicated, however, that so few would be sold that the cost of tooling would not be recovered within the required time limit. Thus, the introduction of ROPS was deferred until 1969, when ROPS became accepted by customers. In the meantime, Oliver engineering participated in the development of the ROPS standards. The specifications became more detailed and complete when the ROPS standard was developed and printed in 1968.

Another major safety issue is the lighting of slow tractors. In 1964, Oliver hosted the FIEI Lighting and Marking Subcommittee meeting in Charles City, Iowa. The purpose was to test proposals by any of the

In November of 1959, Oliver held a show at the Hippodrome in Waterloo, Iowa, to introduce the Model 1800 and 1900 tractors. Dealers were flown in for this event. Model 770 tractors were fitted with power steering and Funk Reversomatic transmissions and were demonstrated in a tractor square dance. In this square dance formation the tractors were driven into the center and back out again, which demonstrated how easy the tractors were to operate, one of Oliver's design criteria for these new tractors. *Chuck Dillman*

Herb Morrell is shown driving the 1900 with a plow into the arena where the dealers viewed the new tractor for the first time. He then presented the specifications and advantages for both the 1800 and 1900 tractors. *Chuck Dillman*

subcommittee members. The Charles City Country Club at Wildwood Park was reserved after sundown to conduct these tests. The Country Club had curves, a hill, a grade and a level road. Distances could be measured under all of these conditions. These tests also included a proposed Slow Moving Vehicle Identification Emblem (SMV) which became ASAE 276 and SAE Standard J943 and was first printed in the 1966 ASAE and SAE Handbooks as a standard.

Introduction of the 1800 Series

The 1800 and 1900 tractors were introduced in November 1959 at the Hippodrome in Waterloo, Iowa. All of the dealers were flown to Waterloo in groups, each group for a two-day meeting. The sales department had changed its attitude regarding the merits of these new tractors, and the 1800 and 1900 tractors and implements were presented successfully.

The show opened with a "square dance" of eight Charles City housewives driving tractors that were equipped with power steering, our regular six-speed tractor transmission, and the Funk Reversomatic between the flywheel and the transmission, which allowed the tractors to be shifted into any one of their speeds. A separate lever was used to change

Since 1960 was an election year, the theme, "Vote for Power" was used to promote Oliver tractors. This was a "demonstration" in the Hippodrome to emphasize this theme for the dealers. The dealers were then invited to view Oliver's new products. *Chuck Dillman*

Draft control was one of the most important features of the new series of models. Here Bob Johnstone of the South Bend Plant explains the two-point draft control hitch on the five-bottom semi-mounted plow to three dealers. *Chuck Dillman*

from reverse to forward. This allowed easy maneuverability, which was dramatically demonstrated by the beautiful young women dressed in western style in Oliver colors driving the tractors in the square dance.

"Most vigorous applause of the evening was given the feminine drivers, costumed in western style and Oliver colors. The women have been practicing the driving patterns for almost three months," wrote the *Charles City Press* on November 12, 1959.

The 1800 and 1900 tractors were then driven into the arena by Walt Gardner and me. After my presentation, and the presentations of others, there was a demonstration of Oliver personnel campaigning to elect these two new model tractors into the Oliver line in the "Vote for Power" campaign. Then the dealers were invited to view the new 1800 and 1900 tractors and updated products from the other Oliver plants.

We announced at the meeting that these new tractors would be available for sale by the middle of 1960. The size of the production run was increased three times by the middle of 1961 and the quantity of four-wheel-drive tractors sold exceeded everyone's expectations.

These larger tractors were difficult to steer manually. In most conditions they required too much effort for the operator and the universal joint angles

In the late 1950s, newly developed implements began to require a higher PTO speed than the standard 540 rpm, so the a new standard of 1,000 rpm was established. An example is this PTO-driven sickle mower on the 1966 1650.

Testing

The first field tests were on farms near Charles City. One experimental model was tested near Lubbock, Texas. There were other tests on the 1800 and 1900 near Clarksdale, Mississippi. Neither of these areas were good remote test areas because the number of hours of operation within one year was limited. Some tests were at Green Giant near Le Sueur, Minnesota, in the summer. Green Giant used the tractors almost 24 hours a day, and often had to plow in the rain and with water running in the furrow to keep up with its farm schedules. The company used one 1900 1,000 hours during a 1,200-hour period.

The experimental 1800 and 1900 tractors had two major and one minor redesign that resulted from the field and laboratory tests. We received many helpful comments from the users of the experimental tractors during the years 1955 to 1959.

exceeded their capacity. So, Oliver offered power steering for both the 1800 and 1900.

Setbacks

The 1800 and 1900 development program had some setbacks. Our development budget was cut because 1956 was not a good sales year, so we could not make any more experimental parts. We could only do design work and follow the field tests of the experimental tractors already built. Also, the Oliver sales department in our Chicago office was not in favor of the 1800 and 1900 program. They said that these new tractors cost too much and could not be sold in large quantities. Then, 1958 was another year of low sales and we had to cut our budget again. We could, however, redesign and test updated experimental models.

During the middle of 1958, we were approaching the release of all of the drawings for the 1800 and 1900 tractor production. One morning, Oliver CEO Alva Phelps and President Carl Hecker flew by company plane from Chicago to Charles City. Plant manager George Bird picked them up at the airport and all three came to the engineering conference room. Carl Hecker said, "This meeting won't take long. We are canceling the X89 or 1800 and 1900 program."

George Bird's answer was, "Before we make a final decision, let's go out and see an 1800 plowing in comparison with the latest J. I. Case tractor and plow." The 1800 was plowing about 25 percent faster with one more plow blade than the J. I. Case tractor and plow. George Bird asked Phelps to ride with him in his air-conditioned Cadillac. They followed the two tractors for about 30 minutes. When they returned to the end of the field, Phelps got out of the car and said to Hecker, "We can't cancel this program because it could be Oliver's salvation."

Certified Horsepower

During the early 1960s, the Oliver tractor plant was criticized because the horsepower quoted for our tractors was not as high as some competing tractors of similar size. The difference was that Oliver quoted the horsepower of the actual production tractors; some competitors only published the horsepower determined by Nebraska test results. The Nebraska test tractor was generally tuned to provide the absolute maximum horsepower, which was higher than tractors could produce under normal operation by customers.

To provide information to Oliver salesmen and dealers, a "Certified Horsepower" decal was placed on the sheet metal on the left side of the tractor. This decal gave the horsepower of that particular tractor when it was assembled and tested. Tractors usually produced greater horsepower after they are broken in than at the time of assembly. The "Certified Horsepower" decal related that this tractor would produce the listed horsepower or more when broken in.

Further Model Upgrades

The frequent upgrading of the tractors and change of model numbers continued through the 1550, 1650, 1750, 1850, and 1950. The next upgrading and model change became the 1555, 1655, 1755, 1855, and 1955.

The versatility of the 1800 and 1900 stemmed from the Fleetline tractors. When the 1600 was introduced in 1962, it became very popular. Not more than six months later, I received requests for approval of two special tractors in one day. A visit with Morrie Thelen of our specifications department revealed that we had approved 1,172 different 1600 tractors. I asked him to tell me how many tractors could be assembled without

This advertisement from 1969 touts features found on the 1750 and 1850. The tilting and telescoping steering wheel, comfortable seat, and cab options added up to increased operator comfort. *Floyd County Historical Society*

During 1967, the Oliver sales department suggested the development of an over and under auxiliary drive known as Hyraul-Shift. Coupled with the standard six-speed transmission, the feature essentially gave the tractor 18 forward speeds. This feature was introduced on the 1650 through 1850 tractors. *J.C. Allen & Son*

designing a new part. He came back with the answer of more than 2.6 million. Oliver had become a truly custom-built tractor company.

Six-cylinder Engines in Agricultural Tractors

The six-cylinder engines introduced in 1935 by Oliver were smooth running, with less vibration than engines having fewer cylinders. International Harvester introduced a new agricultural tractor in 1960 at the Ohio State Fair in Columbus. A large banner at the display featured "Six-Cylinder Smooth Power." John Deere also introduced its new six-cylinder 4010 the same year. The inference was that this was something new in agricultural tractors, but the Oliver 70 in 1935 had a six-cylinder engine. In fact, Oliver had introduced five different models with six-cylinder engines during the 25-year period since then. Oliver's counter advertising program, "Six for a Quarter," consisted of 12,000 folders with cut-outs for six nickels that were sold for 25 cents. This meant "six-cylinder engines for a quarter of a century."

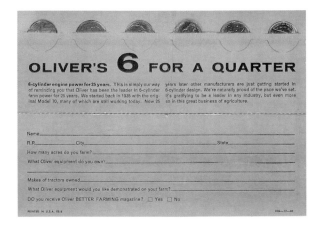

Gasoline and diesel six-cylinder engines were available for the Oliver 1750. The 310-cubic-inch Oliver diesel was good for 80.05 PTO and 65.28 drawbar horsepower in a 1967 Nebraska tractor test. The 283-cubic-inch gasoline version of the 1750, also tested in 1967, produced 80.31 PTO and 67.05 drawbar horsepower *J.C. Allen & Son*

The "Six for a Quarter" promotion was introduced to emphasize that, in 1960, Oliver had been building six-cylinder tractors for a quarter of a century. This Oliver advertising campaign countered John Deere's introduction of their six-cylinder tractor as if it were something new. *Robert Tallman collection*

OLIVER'S 6 FOR A QUARTER

6-cylinder engine power for 25 years. This is simply our way of reminding you that Oliver has been the leader in 6-cylinder farm power for 25 years. We started back in 1935 with the original Model 70, many of which are still working today. Now 25 years later other manufacturers are just getting started in 6-cylinder design. We're naturally proud of the pace we've set. It's gratifying to be a leader in any industry, but even more so in this great business of agriculture.

Name_____

R.R._____ City_____ State_____

How many acres do you farm?_____

What Oliver equipment do you own?_____

Makes of tractors owned_____

What Oliver equipment would you like demonstrated on your farm?_____

DO you receive Oliver BETTER FARMING magazine? ☐ Yes ☐ No

LEFT: The 1850 was available in two- and four-wheel-drive versions, equipped with a 352-cubic-inch Perkins diesel or 310-cubic-inch gasoline engine. Tested at Nebraska in 1964, the gas engine produced 92.43 PTO horsepower, with the diesel cranking out 92.92. *J.C. Allen & Son*

A 1965 Model 1950 with a GM 453 diesel engine. The 1950 could be had in two- or four-wheel-drive. The GM engine produced 105.79 PTO horsepower.

The 1900 series of Oliver tractors were Wheatland tractors with increased power to drive greater than 100 horsepower PTO implements. The rollover protective structure was first designed to be introduced in 1960, but was deferred until later when it was accepted by customers. This is a 1965 Model 1950.

The Model 1950 was tested at Nebraska in 1964. The GM two-cycle diesel engine produced 105.79 maximum horsepower. The tractor weighed in at 11,955 pounds without ballast. The Hydra-Power-equipped tractor pulled 8,996 pounds and produced 98.00 drawbar horsepower.

Auxiliary Transmissions

Oliver built a number of different auxiliary transmissions, all of which provided a range of speeds for each gear in the standard transmission. The operator could shift this auxiliary transmission, and increase or decrease speed and pulling power. The first one used was the Power Booster Drive, which was not a success for Oliver. Most of these units were removed from Oliver tractors.

The next system was Hydra Power Drive, an oil-cooled auxiliary that provided a lower range for extra pulling power in each gear. It was designed and released in 1962.

Over and Under Hydraul-Shift

During the late 1960s, the Oliver sales department suggested the development of an over and under auxiliary drive. The basic tractor transmission could be shifted to any of six speeds. The control lever on the Hydraul-Shift could be moved to overdrive in any of the six speeds, which would increase tractor speed by approximately 15 percent and reduce pulling power by the same 15 percent. The control lever could also be shifted to underdrive to reduce speed by 15 percent and increase power by that same amount. The effect of this feature essentially gave the tractor 18 forward speeds.

The meeting of the standards committee, which developed the Slow Moving Vehicle (SMV) triangular safety emblem was hosted by the Charles City Oliver engineering department. Various designs for safety equipment were specified by the committee and constructed for testing by the Oliver's experimental engineering personnel.

Implements

The implement plants were also innovative and made contributions to agriculture and society. The Oliver South Bend, Indiana, plant developed the throwaway Raydex Shares, a straight-nosed, more simple design of the plowshare. Other plowshares, which had long snouts that were easily bent or broken, were more complicated and costly to maintain. In contrast, the Raydex Shares were disposable, which lowered the cost of maintaining the plows. Oliver also made this implement for Ford.

The Shelbyville plant developed and patented an automatic bale thrower that threw bales of hay into a wagon without the aid of a second person. A license agreement to make this bale thrower was issued to at least one other company.

The development of the Rollover Protective Structure (ROPS) is an example of Oliver's commitment to the safety of the operator. Although the ROPS was designed to be introduced with the 1800 series in 1960, there were indications that customers would not pay the extra cost involved, so the release was delayed until several years later. This is a 1969 Model 2150 diesel.

A four-wheel-drive Oliver Model 1950 diesel pulling some kind of soil preparation device and a sprayer behind; working on bare field. Tractor has badging for Hydra-Power Drive. *J.C. Allen & Son*

The Italian-built Model 1250 was constructed for Oliver by Fiat. This ad features Oliver's "Certified Horsepower" promotion, in which the actual horsepower of the tractor was recorded and marked.

OLIVER 1250, brisk and agile for choring

You couldn't pick a better chore boy than this one—the nimble 1250 that zips through farmstead tasks for pennies in upkeep cost. It's powered right, sized right to do anything, go anywhere. Oliver advancements enable you to save time at every turn. You can

shift on the fly. A differential lock takes you through slippery spots without spinning out. And, there are conveniences galore. Foot accelerator, hand emergency brake, optional power steering. All are yours in the all-purpose 1250. It's the big bargain in the utility tractor line-up.

Certified Horsepower, an Oliver Exclusive

Look for this horsepower certification emblem—found only on Oliver tractors. Here's assurance that you'll get all the punch and productivity potential you pay for, that your new 1250 will deliver its rated horsepower. Here's more than a promise of power—here's proof of power. Take the guesswork out of tractor buying—buy an Oliver and be sure.

ABOVE AND LEFT: This 4-115 White-Oliver four-wheel-drive industrial tractor is powered by a GM 453 engine.

SPECIALTY TRACTORS

Oliver 25 Airport Tractor

Even before the introduction of the Fleetline, Oliver tractors had special uses. For example, the Oliver 25 was a Model 70 tractor with special tires and a special drawbar and hitch for towing small planes, cargo, and other airport materials. This tractor was used by a large number of airports during World War II. When larger planes were developed after World War II, larger and more specialized equipment was needed to perform the same functions.

Military Standardized Engines

After the Korean War, the tractor industry considered the standardization of the engine parts subject to high wear and early replacement, such as connecting rod bearings, main bearings, valves, and other parts. Waukesha Motor and Oliver participated in a standardization program for gasoline engines. There was a demand, at that time, for a large number of tractors to perform maintenance in the U.S. military installations around the world. From 1953 to 1955, Oliver received some of these tractor orders which specified a military standard engine. Some competitors took exception to the military

standard engine and bid tractors at a much lower price. Oliver bid on some proposals with the military standard engine and with the regular commercial tractor engine. Oliver made little or no profit for all of its efforts to provide military tractors.

Alcohol Tractors

During the early 1950s, the country of Formosa, now Taiwan, wanted tractors that would burn pure grain alcohol that could be produced easily from sugar cane. Gasoline was difficult for the country to get, and it was expensive. Some previous grain alcohol tests had been conducted on Oliver's 77 gasoline engine at Waukesha Motor, so we started a program to use the same carburetor with some modifications on an Oliver 77 tractor. Meanwhile, Oliver sent a bid to Formosa and was selected for the contract. We learned quickly, however, that the many restrictions on obtaining pure grain alcohol in the United States made it difficult for us to continue our work. We filled out many forms and wrote many letters about our use of the alcohol and how we would control it. By the time we got through all the red tape required to get alcohol for testing, Formosa had solved its problem and

Oliver tractors were adapted in many ways for a wide variety of tasks. Oliver offered their tractors without wheels as a Power-Pak for other manufacturers to adapt for special applications. This machine is based on a 1953 Super 66 Power-Pak.

ABOVE: The versatility of the Oliver 70 tractor made it easy to customize for special applications. The Model 25 Airport tractor is one example. *Floyd County Historical Society*

was able to get gasoline at a reasonable price, so the Formosa project was canceled.

Special 66 Diesels for Banana Fields

We received an inquiry from banana companies in Guatemala asking if we could provide 50 diesel tractors that had no electrical system. They were having trouble maintaining the batteries and were losing gasoline from their gasoline tractors in the humid, tropical climate.

One cannot hand crank a diesel engine unless it has some kind of compression release. No type of hand cranking of even a small diesel engine has been satisfactory because of the high compression ratio. We located a source that manufactured hydraulic starters and designed a system that included a hand pump and an accumulator to store a volume of hydraulic fluid at high pressures. Approximately 50 strokes of the hand lever were required to build enough fluid and pressure in the accumulator to rotate the engine at 450 rpm for one to three revolutions. This was enough to start the 66 diesel tractors under tropical conditions.

The tractors were used primarily for pulling banana carts from the fields of banana trees. The banana companies liked the units, but Oliver did not get any repeat orders because the workers objected to the hand pump.

A 1953 Super 66 Wheel Roller.

This 1953 Super 66 Wheel Roller, one of two known to exist, is based on an Oliver Power-Pak. It is still in use more than 40 years after it was built and sold.

Remote-controlled Tractors

On the Morrell family farm in eastern Kansas, we had an Avery tractor built in Peoria, Illinois. It was purchased about 1914 for belt work to power a rock crusher, since our family was also in the concrete construction business. This tractor had two speeds, forward 1 3/4 and 2 2/3 miles per hour, and it could pull a two-blade plow. This tractor was used for many years to build silos, chicken houses, water reservoirs, and barns. The tractor finally wore out, and it was difficult to get repair parts. A new Avery tractor was purchased about 1920, and the old one was kept for parts.

In 1924, my brother Paul put a furrow guide on the new Avery tractor. The furrow guide consisted of a wheel in front of the tractor's right front wheel that was connected to the tractor steering mechanism. The guide wheel would follow the furrow and guide the tractor without an operator.

One Saturday we took a car and saddle horse to the field, along with the tractor and plow. While the tractor was plowing without an operator, Paul was fixing the car. When the tractor neared the other end of the field, Paul rode the horse to the tractor, turned it around, and started it plowing back toward the car. He then rode the horse back to the car. When the tractor neared our end of the field, Paul turned it around and started toward the other end of the field. Paul then could get more work done fixing the car. The tractor was operated in the lowest gear of 1 3/4 miles per hour. It seemed that it took forever to plow that field. My function was to watch the tractor and hand tools to Paul when he asked for them. This was quite an experience for me at eight years of age.

The Avery tractor was difficult to start when the temperature was lower than 45 degrees F. We had a large draft horse named Mace that was not nervous around machinery. On some of these cold occasions, Paul wrapped a rope around the flywheel and tied the other end of the rope to a single tree hitched to the tugs of Mace's harness. Mace was then led and the rope rotated the flywheel. This was a great idea until one day the tractor backfired and dragged Mace backward. After that incident, poor old Mace refused to pull the rope to start the tractor.

During the early 1950s, Oliver started a research project to control a tractor from a remote position. A graduate student at the University of Nebraska had started the project with radio controls.

He came to Charles City and worked with Charlie Adams in our experimental engineering department to apply the radio controls to an Oliver 88 tractor. Using the remote radio control, the tractor engine could be started; transmission gears shifted; the engine speed increased and decreased; the clutch engaged and disengaged; the tractor steered; implements lifted and lowered; left, right, or both brakes applied; the tractor stopped; and the ignition turned off.

Tampo Pneumatic Road Roller units were built using Oliver Power-Paks. On the left is a small unit with a gasoline engine. In the center is a larger unit with a diesel engine, and the large unit using a twin 880 Power-Pak is on the right. *Carl Rabe*

An Oliver 50-based road grader. *J.C. Allen & Son*

129

This Oliver 66 Military tractor was equipped with the required standard engine parts. The tractor with a hydraulic mower was used for mowing in and around military installations. *Carl Rabe*

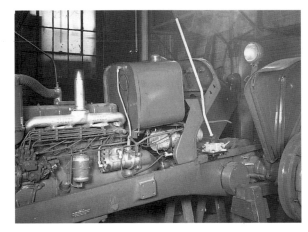

Banana plantations were experiencing problems maintaining the batteries and other electrical devices in the tropical climate, so they asked Oliver to develop a tractor with no electrical system. This shows a 66 tractor with a unique, non-electric, hydraulic starter installed. The long lever was used to manually recharge the hydraulic oil accumulator. *Carl Rabe*

Industrial tractors equipped with hydraulic mowers were important for special mowing requirements. Their flexibility, rugged construction, and hydraulic drive provided good results. This shows an Oliver Industrial Model 550 with a hydraulic mower. *C. J. Gibbs*

This Super 77 was equipped with a Danco rotary mower and chains to meet the Kansas Turnpike Authority's specifications The mesh screens were added so the mowers would not throw up rocks onto the passing vehicles. These bright yellow and blue tractors could be seen for many years alongside the Kansas Turnpike. *Carl Rabe*

The radio-controlled tractor really worked. It was a novel idea to sit at the end of a field and operate the tractor by remote control, but it had some disadvantages. The tractor had to remain within sight, making it impractical in extremely large or hilly fields, while precision cultivating or in other such conditions. Still, we learned much from this research project.

Oliver engineering never felt that a remote-control agricultural tractor was practical. Since that time, there has been research on providing guide wires in the soil for the tractor to follow using radio control, but there is no consideration to my knowledge of further development of this system because it would be costly to install and maintain, and would have a very low payback.

Industrial Tractors with Hydraulic Mowers

The Industrial 66, 77, and 88 tractors with hydraulic mowers were other special tractor combinations. The mower was driven by a hydraulic system driven by the tractor engine. The mower was powerful and could cut small trees up to about an inch in diameter.

Several of us from Oliver visited an unusual area where the tractor with mower was demonstrated. This was on a mountain plateau near Archbald, Pennsylvania, northwest of Scranton. A tractor with a hydraulic mower had been loaned to the owner of the plateau to mow brush that was killing the wild blueberry plants. The owner had attached a wick-like set of ribbons that was soaked in a poison to kill the approximately 6-inch-high brush stumps. If this tractor and mower worked, the owner planned to buy about 20 industrial tractors with hydraulic mowers to mow the brush on several thousand acres of the plateau.

The owner also had an apple-processing plant that supplied apple slices to bakeries in New York City and other large cities in that area. He used a toxic chemical to keep the apple slices looking freshly cut when being transported from his plant. The last information I received was that the tractor and mower had been picked up and the owner of the plateau was in prison for his use of toxic chemicals.

Super 77s for the Kansas Turnpike Authority

The Kansas Turnpike Authority was responsible for the construction and maintenance of the

Kansas Turnpike, and it needed tractors. To meet specifications, Oliver worked with mower manufacturer Danco of Claremore, Oklahoma.

The Super 77 adjustable front-axle tractor was chosen. The plans included 6-foot-wide rotary mower units to be mid-mounted between the front and rear wheels and driven by the independent power take-off on the tractor. The mower had to meet certain specifications to prevent the throwing of debris, such as beer bottles, at passing vehicles. Many types of discharge guards were tried to meet the Kansas Turnpike specifications. We finally put log chain links over the mower openings to prevent rocks, glass, and other debris from being thrown at passing vehicles. The final test included the mowing of some scrub oak

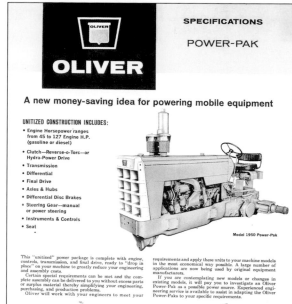

The Oliver Power-Pak was very popular for many applications. Most companies purchased engines, transmissions, and other parts from Oliver to assemble their own units. *Carl Rabe*

The Cleveland Tractor Company was founded in 1916. It built crawlers right from the start and, by the late 1920s, had a full line of crawlers from the 10- to the 55-horsepower range. This example is a 1950 Cletrac Model HG.

The Cletrac Model HG was introduced in 1939. It used a Hercules four-cylinder engine. Oliver continued production of this model through 1951.

trees and bushes. Any tree that could be bent down by the tractor's front axle had to be mowed down and reduced to wood chips.

The tractors were painted dark blue and bright yellow, as specified by the Kansas Turnpike Authority. Whenever we traveled the Kansas Turnpike, we saw these tractors in operation or parked on the right-of-way.

Numerous other companies adapted their products to Oliver's Fleetline tractors. Arps made a trencher and Sherman a backhoe, and there are no doubt many more. These special tractors helped to keep

the Charles City tractor plant open during low sales of conventional agricultural and industrial tractors.

Oliver Power-Pak

During the middle- to late-1950s, Oliver produced the Power-Pak, which allowed other companies to use Oliver's versatility and excellent designs for their own applications. This "unitized construction" included a gasoline or diesel engine, clutch or "Reverse-a-Torc" transmission, differential, final drive, axles and hubs, double-disc brakes, steering gear with power steering option, instruments, controls, and seat.

By the time Oliver purchased Cletrac in 1944, Cletrac had an amazing range of crawlers, including the more than 27,000-pound, 100-plus-horsepower Model F series machines. This 1950 Cletrac HG was designed for orchard and farm work.

Powered by a 895-cubic-inch Hercules six-cylinder diesel engine and weighing in at more than 16 1/2 tons, the OC-18 produced 133 drawbar horsepower. This is a 1952 Oliver OC-18 crawler tractor.

The powerful OC-18 could pull more than 31,000 pounds at the drawbar. Oliver quit producing crawlers in 1965.

FAR RIGHT: This 1958 Cletrac OC-4 crawler tractor and loader is still at work. The OC-4 had a 130-cubic-inch Hercules three-cylinder engine available in gasoline- or diesel-burning configurations.

Pneumatic Road Roller Units

Oliver Power-Paks were used to power pneumatic road roller units that compacted the soil for road and highway construction. Oliver worked with Ferguson of Dallas, Texas, and Tampo in San Antonio, Texas, to provide the power and the propelling device in Oliver Power-Pak units prepared for this application. These units consisted of the basic tractor minus the front and rear wheels and tires. Special axles were provided so that the road roller could be driven by using sprockets and chains from the tractor axles. Other companies, such as Bros, also manufactured road roller units that used the Oliver Power-Pak.

Twin 880 Tractors

The Euclid Division of General Motors had a crawler tractor with two engines and two transmissions mounted on the same frame. Each unit drove one of the two tracks. The twin combination was very powerful as a bulldozer and in doing other types of similar work. George Bird, our plant manager, was intrigued with Euclid's twin unit. He always showed great interest in anything new or novel. He reasoned that Oliver could make a special unit with twice the power of the 880. We tried to discourage him from pursuing such a project without a market survey. But we agreed to submit a development project to build one unit and then evaluate the usage later.

In November 1958, I was scheduled to be gone for two weeks to check on the inventory of a large number of attachments for Oliver industrial tractors that had been purchased for the industrial sales department. Before I left, we had a staff meeting to establish what was to be accomplished while I was gone. When I returned home and reviewed the status of each project, I found that nothing had been accomplished on the assigned projects. Each project engineer had been reassigned to the design of the Twin 880 by George Bird. The result was that some critical engineering projects had been delayed.

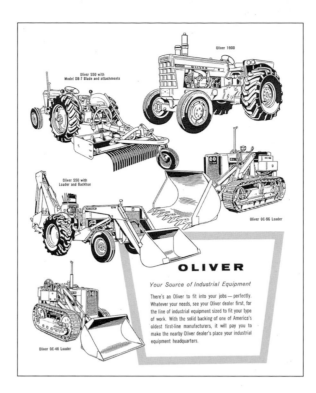

This advertisement shows a variety of Oliver models offered with loaders and other implements. "There's an Oliver to fit into your jobs—perfectly. Whatever your needs, see your Oliver dealer first, for the line of industrial equipment sized to fit your type of work." *Bob Tallman collection*

Lull's Model 7C used a 770 Power-Pak. These were sold in reasonable quantities for two or three years. The unit was valuable for constructing houses or other low buildings. *Courtesy of Glenn B. Bazen, Lull collection*

For taller, commercial construction, Lull designed a heavy High-Lift Loader with four-wheel drive. This unit was upgraded many times to meet the requirements of larger construction sites. *Courtesy of Glenn B. Bazen, Lull collection*

ing gates before the horses came back around the track. Another unit was sold for pulling a "sheep's foot roller" used for compaction in highway construction. A third Twin 880 Power-Pak was used in a Tampo pneumatic road roller. The other Twin 880s were disassembled and the parts were used to assemble regular 880 tractors.

Crawler Tractors

During the early days of crawler tractor production, the Cletrac, made by the Cleveland Tractor Company, was rated among the best. The Cleveland Tractor Company was started in 1917 as the Cleveland Motor Plow Company and was purchased by Oliver in 1944. The industrial sales were controlled by the Cletrac Sales Department. Their main emphasis for many years was on crawler tractors and attachments, such as front-mounted loaders. Cletrac models continued to be produced at the Cleveland plant until 1963, when that plant was closed and the crawler tractor production was moved to Charles City.

Lull Loaders

Oliver had a special working relationship with Lull Engineering of St. Paul, Minnesota, which became an original equipment manufacturer using Oliver's basic tractor units. Lull was one of the first to produce front-end loaders for Oliver's Industrial 80 tractor and then made a front-end loader for early Oliver 88 Industrial tractors.

Lull also made a high-lift loader used to place construction material on the second and third floors of a building under construction. The first high-lift loader, the Model 58, was built around an Oliver 66 tractor. The tractor provided the power and the drive mechanism. Lull designed a frame to accept the modified 66 tractor. Special hydraulics, a lift mechanism, and other assemblies were required by Lull to complete the vehicle. The Model 58 High-Lift Loader was able to lift 2,000 pounds to a height of 22 1/5 feet. This unit was helpful on smaller construction jobs, but there was a need for higher lifts.

Later, Lull's Model 7C used an Oliver 770 engine, transmission, and final drive. It was able to lift 3,000 pounds to a height of 40 feet. Since the 7C, Lull High-Lift Loaders have developed into much larger and higher capacity units. Lull then began to purchase four-wheel-drive axles, engines, transmissions,

Six Twin 880 units were built. One Twin 880 was demonstrated at the Oliver International show in Libertyville, Illinois, in June 1959. Sam White Jr., president of Oliver International, was the master of ceremonies for the program. He introduced George Bird, who talked briefly about the Twin 880 unit. Foreign countries showed no interest in it.

One Twin 880 was sold to the Santa Anita racetrack in California to remove the horse race start-

hydraulic components, and then build the frame and other necessary parts to complete the vehicle.

Ware Machine Works

Ware Machine Works of Ware, Massachusetts, made a front-end loader and a backhoe for the Industrial 88. John Pilch, owner of Ware, became quite interested in the new 88 with its advanced design and versatility. He was partly responsible for getting the Oliver Industrial wheel tractors promoted through Oliver's industrial sales department.

John Pilch started his business in textile plants that were vacated after the companies moved south to the Carolinas and Virginia for low cost of

labor and fewer union problems. My visits to his plant were always stimulating. During each visit, he would go to his file and pull out a patent on some new device that he had invented. We usually did some brainstorming on other possible tractor attachments that would be worthwhile to pursue.

His hospitality was great! He provided sleeping accommodations at his retreat home in the mountains nearby. Once he gave me a fishing pole and two worms, saying, "You are going to catch the fish for our supper." I went to a large pond nearby and easily caught several catfish of good eating size. It seems that John often fed his fish, and they were eager to bite on most anything thrown to them, including a bare hook.

One of my visits was during the fur trapping season. John insisted on getting some of his friends together to go coon hunting that evening. He had hunting outfits of all sizes in his mountain home. We hunted until midnight and then had a snack before retiring. We were tired from following the dogs on the trail of a smart coon. The coon went in and out of streams of water and a small lake several times to decoy the dogs into the water. A coon can drown a dog in the water. The coon finally ended up in a large

The Ware Loader was a popular implement for the Oliver Model 70 Industrial tractor. *Floyd County Historical Society*

LEFT BELOW: The Twin 880 was another Oliver experiment. In theory, such a unit sounded promising. Oliver engineers traveled extensively, but they found no market for a twin unit. It was limited to pulling implements such as this sheep foot roller.

The Lull Loader on a Super 88 tractor is typical of the front-end loaders for the Industrial 77 and 88 tractor series. These front-end loaders provided a good start for Oliver's Industrial tractors. *Courtesy of Glenn B. Bazen, Lull collection*

This Super 55 with a forklift attached was used to move materials at the Oliver plant through snow and other poor traction conditions. It was quite successful commercially. *Carl Rabe*

New styling and better stability when lifting maximum loads made the 552 an improvement over the already very successful Super 55. *Floyd County Historical Society*

oak tree still full of its fall leaves. There was no way that we could get the coon out of this tree. While we were having our snack, John's oldest and wisest dog, Queeny, treed another coon within 100 yards of his mountain home. The next night, we had coon for dinner, which was specially prepared by one of John's expert cooks.

John's company developed high-capacity hydraulic pumps that could be mounted on the front, driven from the engine's crankshaft, or mounted on the rear of the Industrial 88, driven by the independent power take-off.

Ware's large backhoe provided good productivity for city service installations of sewers and utilities. It quickly became popular for many other earthmoving applications. In fact, the Ware backhoe set a standard for many others to follow. Ware continued to manufacture backhoes and loaders exclusively for Oliver tractors.

The Parsons Company of Newton, Iowa, made some loaders and backhoes of lower capacity than the Ware units. They were adaptable to the medium-size tractors, such as Oliver's Industrial 77.

Danuser Machine Works of Fulton, Missouri, made a line of three-point hitch-mounted scrapers, landscaping blade, and other landscaping implements and attachments for light industrial wheel tractors. These were to be used with Oliver's Industrial wheel tractors.

Maine Strait-Line Loader

Maine Steel Company of Portland, Maine, had an interesting loader designed especially to be attached to an Oliver Industrial 88. This loader was unique in that the bucket could be loaded or emptied from the front or rear of the tractor and transported from the front to the rear. The advantage in this design was more productivity. One could run the tractor in a straight line to load and empty without having to turn the tractor around, saving much steering and shifting of gears. Under some conditions, the Strait-Line Loader could load gravel from a pit two or three times as fast as a conventional loader.

The main disadvantage of the Strait-Line loader was evident when it was operated on a slope or rough terrain. It was not very stable when the load was being transported from front to rear and vice versa. A small number were sold for special applications. Most of the owners were happy with the increased productivity. But just as we were getting started with this unit, George Soule, the owner, was having difficulty with the Internal Revenue Service. He had deducted the cost of development from the company's income taxes, but the Internal Revenue Service ruled that the development was productive work that increased his property, and the deductions were not allowed. Soule was forced into bankruptcy, ending another interesting adventure.

Super 55 and 552 Forklift

The versatile Super 55 and 550 became important material-handling units. The typical industrial forklift tractor was ineffective at moving material in snow, soft ground, or in other poor traction conditions. The K-D Manufacturing Company of Waco, Texas, made forklift towers. The differential drive behind the transmission on the Oliver Super 55 and 550 tractors could be assembled to provide six speeds in reverse and two forward speeds. This was accomplished by placing the large differential spiral bevel gear on the other side of the spiral bevel pinion. The tractor controls and the operator's seat were assembled so that the operator faced the rear of the tractor. The K-D forklift tower was mounted next to the large driving wheels in front of the reversed operator's position. The Super 55 became quite popular for moving outside material at our plant and at many other storage facilities.

The Super 55 was then improved for better stability under a maximum load and given new styling to become the Model 552. Oliver 552 forklifts were popular for use in outside storage near factories and businesses. Because of the large tires, they were particularly useful in the winter for moving outside material in the snow. The weight of the tower and the load provided good traction in snow, ice, and on soft ground.

The Davis Manufacturing Company of Wichita, Kansas, made smaller loaders and backhoes to fit smaller tractors, such as the Oliver Super 55 and 550 models.

Lull Street Sweeper

During the late 1950s, Lull Engineering adapted an Oliver 550 tractor as a road and street sweeper, the Model SP-2A Road and Street Broom. The 550 tractor's operator position and controls were reversed. The engine then had no axle or support under it. The broom and the frame were behind the drive wheels and the tractor was driven backwards. The spiral bevel gear could be positioned on the other side of the spiral bevel pinion to provide six speeds in reverse and two forward. The position of the engine provided good fore and aft stability.

An interesting problem developed when Lull Engineering decided to add water tanks to the tractor. These water tanks provided water for sprinkling to overcome dusty conditions. The extra 3,000 pounds of water on the rear axles caused some axle failures. Adding the water tanks

had not been reviewed with Oliver engineering.

The axle failures led Lull to believe that Oliver did not have the strongest axle construction. We suggested that an immediate solution would be to put trusses under the axles and rear tractor frame, but Lull used Oliver's rear-axle drawing and attempted to make some axles according to his own theory. His axles failed so quickly that he came back to us for assistance in the design of the trusses. The trusses were satisfactory, and to my knowledge, Lull experienced no serious failures.

Another good use of the 550 was in the Lull Street Sweeper. The versatility of the 550 provided an ideal reverse-driven Power-Pak for sweeper application. *Courtesy of Glenn B. Bazen, Lull collection*

These Super 88s are equipped with Lull Loaders and dual rear wheels.

Massey-Ferguson contracted with Oliver to make a large tractor for them until they were ready to produce their own. The Oliver 990 was the right size and power to meet the company's general specifications, so it was used to produce the Massey-Ferguson 98 standard tractor. *Carl Rabe*

990 and 995 Scrapers

The 990 and 995 Scrapers were additional special units for earth moving. The scraper attachment was manufactured by a company in Columbia, South Carolina. This was a project managed at Oliver's tractor plant in South Bend. Several of these units were sold to a road construction company that built "side boards" for the scraper. The side boards greatly increased the capacity of the scraper, but these scraper units were abused by their owner. The construction company went bankrupt, and the units were repossessed, rebuilt, and sold as used equipment.

Hancock Scraper

The Hancock Scraper Company of Lubbock, Texas, tested the 1900 tractor without front wheels as a propelling unit for a scraper. During early tests, I received a call from the chief engineer regarding a problem. Some of the capscrews used to attach the axle carrier to the rear frame were loose. He asked, "Could someone from your engineering department

The Oliver 500 was available with a gasoline or diesel engine. The maximum PTO power was estimated at 30 to 33 horsepower. The Model 500 was only produced from 1960 to 1963. *Floyd County Historical Society*

come to Lubbock to observe the problem?" We were in the process of arranging transportation when he called back and said, "Forget my earlier telephone call. I have just returned from the test site. The test unit fell about 24 feet down an almost vertical embankment and remained intact. I am no longer concerned about the strength of your unit."

Massey-Ferguson 98 Tractor

During the late 1950s, Massey-Ferguson looked for some large Wheatland tractors to sell until the company could design and introduce its own large tractor. The company came to Oliver. For Massey-Ferguson we built a tractor with the chassis of the Oliver 990 with a four-cylinder GM diesel engine. The sheet metal, decals, and color were all specified by Massey-Ferguson. Several hundred were manufactured before the introduction of the 1800 and 1900 and before Massey-Ferguson started to manufacture its own large tractors.

David Brown

The market for small tractors changed in the early 1960s. Professional people began buying small farm acreages for building homes. They worked at their regular jobs during the week, and in the evenings and on weekends they farmed at their hobby farm. Small foreign tractors were appealing to them because of their size and lower cost. Roy Randt, manager of product planning at Oliver, negotiated with David Brown of England to sell the David Brown 500 in the United States with Oliver colors, decals, and grilles. This tractor was called the Oliver 500.

Fiat

Oliver's contract with David Brown was canceled when David Brown started selling its tractors in the United States. In 1964, J. D. Wormley, executive vice president of Oliver, started working with Fiat of Italy to establish a new source for small tractors. When I became coordinator of outside products in 1965, the Fiat tractors became my responsibility. The first gasoline 1250 tractors were not satisfactory, so Oliver made a number of suggestions. Fiat redesigned the small tractors, accepting Oliver's suggestions for the new diesel design.

In 1966, the larger Fiat tractor became Oliver's 1450 model. Both the 1250 and 1450 tractors were sent from the plant in Modena, Italy, to Genoa and then by ship to Jacksonville, Florida. Oliver then shipped them to Decatur, Georgia, where American tires and lights were installed and Oliver decals and grilles were added. It was a pleasure to meet Dr. Carneo, president of Fiat, when I was in Italy in November 1969. Fiat became a good source for small Oliver tractors.

The Oliver 1250 was made by Fiat in Italy. It had a certified PTO power of 38.5 horsepower when operated at a maximum speed of 2,500 rpm. This was a very reliable model.

The Oliver 1450 diesel, also made in Italy by Fiat, had an estimated PTO power of 55 horsepower when operated at 1,900 rpm. These tractors were overdesigned, which gave them an extra long lifetime.

TRACTOR MODELS BY HART-PARR AND SUCCESSORS

Hart-Parr Models

Model	Comment	Years Manufactured
17-30*	Nos. 1, 2	1902–1906
22-40		1903–1907
22-45		1908–1911
30-60	"Old Reliable" (on display at Charles City, Iowa)	1911–1916
40-80		1908–1909
15-30		1909–1911
60-100	9-foot-diameter drive wheels	1912
20-40		1911–1914
12-27		1913–1914
15-22	Little Red Devil—single wear drive wheel.	1914–1916
18-35		1914–1918
12-25	First low silhouette tractor, water-cooled.	1918
15-30A		1918–1922
35	Road King—extra lugs for pulling road graders	1919
10-20B		1920–1922
10-20C		1922–1924
15-30C		1922–1924
22-40		1923–1927
16-30E		1924–1925
16-30F		1926
12-24E		1924–1926
18-36G		1926–1927
18-36H		1927–1928
18-36I		1928–1930
28-50		1927–1930
12-24G		1926–1927
12-24H		1927–1930

Oliver/Hart-Parr Models

Model	Comment	Years Manufactured
18-28		1930–1937
18	Industrial (18-28)	1931
28	Industrial (improved 18-28)	1932–1939
18-27	Row Crop—single front wheel	1930–1931
18-27	Row Crop—dual front wheel	1931–1937
28-44		1930–1937
44	Industrial (28-44)	1932–1939

* In these model numbers the first number indicates the rated drawbar horsepower and the second is the rated belt horsepower.

Oliver Models

Model	Comment	Years Manufactured
90 & 99	Standard	1937–1952
35 & 80	Industrial	1939–1947
50 & 99	Industrial	1939–1947
70	Row Crop	1935–1948
70	Standard-Style # 1	1936–1937
70	Standard-Style # 2	1937–1948
70	Orchard	1936–1948
25	Airport (70 Standard)	1937–1948
80	Standard	1937–1948
80	Row Crop	1937–1948
EOA	Engine Over Transmission	1938–1967
60	Row Crop	1940–1948
60	Standard	1942–1948
60	Industrial	1946–1948
900	Industrial	1946–1950

Oliver Models (continued)

Model	Comment	Years Manufactured
66	**Fleetline**—Row Crop	1949–1954
66	**Fleetline**—Standard and Industrial	1949–1954
77	**Fleetline**—Row Crop	1948–1954
77	**Fleetline**—Standard and Industrial	1948–1954
88	**Fleetline**—Row Crop	1947–1954
88	**Fleetline**—Standard and Industrial	1947–1954
99	6-cylinder	1953–1954
Super 55		1954–1958
Super 66		1954–1958
Super 77		1954–1958
Super 88		1954–1958
Super 44		1957–1958
Super 99		1954–1958
550		1958–1975
660		1959–1964
770		1958–1967
880		1958–1963
950		1958–1961
990		1958–1961
995		1958–1961
990 Scraper		1957
995 Scraper		1958
440		1960 & 1962
500	Made by David Brown in England	1960–1964
550 & 551	Forklift	1958–1964
552	Forklift	1965–1967
600	Made by David Brown	1962–1964
1800A		1960–1962
1800B		1962–1963
1800C		1963–1964

Model	Comment	Years Manufactured
1900A		1960–1962
1900B		1962–1963
1900C		1963–1964
1600		1962–1964
1250	Made by Fiat in Italy	1965–1969
1450	Made by Fiat in Italy	1967–1969
1650		1964–1969
1750		1964–1969
1850		1964–1969
1950		1964–1967
1950T		1967–1969
1550		1965–1969
1255	Made by Fiat in Italy	1969–1971
1265	Made by Fiat in Italy	1971–1975
1355	Made by Fiat in Italy	1969–1971
1365	Made by Fiat in Italy	1971–1975
1465	Made by Fiat in Italy	1973–1975
2050		1968–1969
2150		1968–1969
1555		1969–1975
1655		1969–1975
1755		1970–1975
1855		1969–1975
1955		1969–1975
1865	MM G 950	1971
1870	G 955—Made for Cockshutt	1973–1974
2270	G 1355—Made for Cockshutt	1972–1974
2055	MMG 1050 LP gas and diesel	1971
2155	MMG 1350 LP gas and diesel	1971
2255		1972–1975
2455	MM A4T 1400	1970
2655	MM A4T 1600	1971–1972

SAFTEY STANDARDS

One of the most important parts of developing a new line of tractors is to know and understand the technical standards and recommendations that apply to tractors. Standards and recommendations can be effective at reducing injuries and accidents on the farm and in other work places.

Standards also allow interchangeability between tractors and implements made by different manufacturers. During the late 1920s, there were approximately 2,500 special hook-up packages required to fit all power take-off–driven implements to all makes of tractors. Standards and recommendations were established so that by the early 1940s any implement could be hooked up to any tractor without the need for a special package.

Standards Organizations

The standards organizations for farm and light industrial equipment consist of several technical societies. The Society of Automotive Engineers (SAE) is responsible for standards and other documents involving tractors and their components. Other aspects of agriculture and agricultural machinery are covered by the American Society of Agricultural Engineers (ASAE). There are some standards, such as those on the power take-off, that affect both agricultural tractors and implements. Standards in these overlapping areas are established through a cooperative effort between the ASAE and SAE.

The Farm Equipment Institute (FEI) started in 1895 as a manufacturer's trade association. It was later superseded by the Farm and Industrial Equipment Institute (FIEI). FIEI committees were set up to research and propose standards to be published by the

ASAE and SAE. Members of the ASAE and SAE are individual engineers and associates, so they could not commit employer funds and time to develop in-depth proposals. Through FIEI, however, companies could establish engineering projects to cover the funds and the time spent by their employees in the development of standards. Oliver projects contributed as much as $50,000 per year.

Standards issues were considered by the FIEI Advisory Engineering Committee, which generally consisted of the chief tractor engineer and a chief engineer of one implement plant from each farm equipment company. When standards were developed or changed by the committee, they were referred to both the ASAE and SAE. After approval, standards are published in the *ASAE Yearbook* and *SAE Handbook*. Those standards of worldwide significance are also submitted to the American National Standards Institute (ANSI) to be considered by the International Standards Organization (ISO). FIEI since has been replaced by the Equipment Manufacturers Institute.

These organizations have no power to enforce standards, so manufacturers' compliance is voluntary. Adherence to published SAE and ASAE standards is often a factor, however, in product liability lawsuits, so compliance is in the best interest of the manufacturers.

I was deeply involved in the standards activity of the FEI, and later the FIEI, representing Oliver from 1951 to 1970 and Owatonna Manufacturing Company from 1970 to 1977. I also served on numerous committees of the SAE, ASAE, and American National Standards Institute. Standards and recommendations efforts continue to grow and there are a large number of committees active in the 1990s.

California Safety Orders

During the mid-1950s, a long list of safety items was sent from the state of California to FIEI for consideration. It covered such items as stepladders. The Advisory Engineering Committee was assigned to study the items specifically for tractors and implements. Among the items were requests to have all tractors with the same gearshift pattern and controls all located in the same position and actuated in the same direction. After the meeting, Bill Coultas of John Deere said, "The next thing they will want to standardize is the number of engine cylinders." Someone asked him, "How many cylinders would you recommend?" Bill replied, "Any number as long as it is no more than two." Someone then asked, "How about that four-cylinder gasoline engine that you use to start your two-cylinder diesel?" Bill's reply was, "You would have to bring up that thing."

Drawbar and Hitch Standards

One of the first known standards for tractors was the distance between the top of the drawbar and the ground. The standard was originally established in 1917 and was revised in 1937. The revised standard was 12 to 15 inches for tractors with 0 to 50 drawbar horsepower, 14 to 18 inches for tractors with 51 to 125 drawbar horsepower, and 16 to 21 inches for tractors with 126 to 175 drawbar horsepower. The revised standard was jointly adopted by the American Society of Agricultural Engineers (ASAE) and the Society of Automotive Engineers (SAE) in 1937 to be published in their handbooks.

Approximately 40 years later, the three-point hitch standard was approved. This was necessary because of the various sizes of implements. The standard recommends sizes of hitch points so that the hitch and implement have compatible dimensions and enough strength. Besides this interchangeability issue, the standard also addresses a safety issue. Use of the wrong size hitch for a particular implement could create a dangerous situation.

Power Take-off Standards

More effort went into creating power take-off standards than any of the other standards. The first PTO standard was established from a report to the SAE in 1923. The standard consisted of 536 rpm and clockwise rotation when viewed from the rear of the tractor. Wayne Worthington, director of engineering of John Deere, was involved in creating this standard. The ASAE became active in these standards soon after 1924. Splined shafts, dimensions, and other necessary information were added later. W. Leland Zink of the General Implement Company was chairman of the ASAE Power Take-off Committee during the late 1920s. His committee was involved primarily with implements, implement drivelines, and tractor output driveshafts.

The 540-rpm standard PTO could not be used for implements requiring more than 50 horsepower. The shaft would become overloaded and fail easily at power requirements above 50 horsepower. Implements and tractors with more than 50 horsepower were anticipated in the near future. The same diameter shaft of 1 3/8 inches with involute splines and driven at 1,000 rpm could be used up to 100 horsepower. For the larger tractors, a 1 3/4-inch diameter shaft with involute splines and a capacity of 100 to 160 horsepower could be used.

But the 1,000-rpm PTO was not considered effective in 1956. Oliver at Charles City was host to the FIEI subcommittees and the Advisory Engineering Committee during April 1957. Special tractors were prepared by Oliver for the study and review of a 1,000-rpm PTO by the Power Take-Off Subcommittee and the Advisory Engineering Committee. Recommendations were made and the next year the SAE Tractor Technical Committee approved the 1,000-rpm PTO Standard J719.

The driveline between the tractor and the implement is dangerous unless the rotating shaft is well protected by shields. There was a fatal accident at a Floyd County, Iowa, home for the elderly that proved this. The tunnel shields around the driveline had been removed and the operator stepped too close to the shaft, wrapping his coat in it. This occurred in 1958, and at the next meeting of the subcommittee and at the Advisory Engineering Committee, I made a motion to specify the integral rotating shield as a standard. Some objected because the bearings in the rotating shield did not have satisfactory life. I then requested that the chairman of the Subcommittee on Power

Take-off establish a task group to develop standards for bearings. Guests from the integral rotating shield manufacturers were invited to attend the next meeting of the Power Take-off Subcommittee. We received their recommendations, which resulted in greatly improved bearings. This specification of the integral rotating shield within the standard continued until recently.

Lighting and Marking of Farm Equipment

One of my first subcommittee meetings was in 1951 at International Harvester Company's experimental farm in Hinsdale, Illinois. The subcommittee had received some reports of highway accidents between automobiles and slow-moving farm equipment. We reviewed several suggestions and chose a flashing electric light mounted on the left wheel guard that showed amber from the front and red from the rear. But that proposal was unacceptable because the Uniform Vehicle Code reserved flashing red rear lights for emergency vehicles.

The next proposal was a light mounted on the left wheel guard with 15 feet of extra electric wire so that if the light on the tractor was obscured from the rear, the light could be

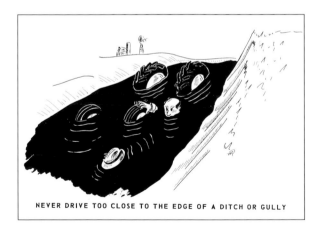

NEVER DRIVE TOO CLOSE TO THE EDGE OF A DITCH OR GULLY

REDUCE SPEED BEFORE TURNING OR USING ONE WHEEL BRAKE

moved to the extreme left side of the implement. This light showed amber from the front and the rear. Specifications from SAE standards were used to create this light.

In 1964, Oliver hosted the FIEI Lighting and Marking Subcommittee meeting in Charles City, Iowa. The purpose was to test proposals by any of the subcommittee members. The Charles City Country Club at Wildwood Park was reserved after sundown to conduct these tests. The country club had curves, a hill, a grade, and a level road. Distances could be measured under all of these conditions. These tests also included a proposed Slow Moving Vehicle (SMV) identification emblem, which became ASAE 276 and SAE Standard J943 and was first printed in the 1966 ASAE and SAE handbooks as a standard.

During the daytime meetings, the subcommittee agreed on which tests to perform each night. The lighting equipment was then assembled by Oliver's experimental engineering department, and the subcommittee reconvened at the country club after dark. On the third night, we tested the equipment on the highway. A tractor with the SMV emblem, red taillight, and two amber flashing lights mounted on the left and right wheel guards was driven on Highway 14 west of Charles City. We were pleased that the traffic slowed and was cautious when approaching the tractor. After these tests were completed, Waldo Seiple of John Deere and I wrote the proposed standard for review at the next subcommittee meeting. The only negative votes were from the members who did not attend the tests at Charles City. The standard was finally printed in the *ASAE Handbook* as S279 and SAE J137 in 1970. Some states do not use these standards but have their own standards. *A Compendium of State Laws Relevant to Farm Equipment*, prepared by FIEI in 1981, shows how state laws vary. This SMV emblem became generally accepted.

Safety Cartoons

Oliver was a leader in the development of technical publications for agricultural equipment. The *Oliver Operator's Manual, Parts List, and Service Manual* were used as models when preparing "ASAE Engineering Practice EP363" and "SAE J1035 Recommended Practice on Technical Publications for Agricultural Equipment." The *Oliver Super 55 Operator's Manual* included safety cartoons drawn by Bill Phillips, an illustrator in the service department in Charles City.

NEVER OPERATE THE ENGINE IN A CLOSED GARAGE OR SHED

BE SURE GEAR SHIFT IS IN NEUTRAL BEFORE STARTING ENGINE

DEVELOPMENT OF OLIVER'S NEW GASOLINE ENGINE

By T.H. Morrell, Chief Engineer
and K.S. Minard, Project Engineer
Oliver Corporation, Charles City, Iowa

**Presented at the Heavy Duty
Vehicle Meeting
Milwaukee, Wisconsin
Sept. 11-14, 1961**

*Reprinted with Permission from SAE
Paper No. 610385 © 1961
Society of Automotive Engineers, Inc.*

Abstract

After completion of XO-121 development (12:1 compression ratio for a tractor engine) and additional studies by Ethyl Corporation, development was continued on Oliver's family of gasoline engines. An important objective was to improve power and economy through better utilization of fuel qualities by finding optimum design combinations for current and projected fuels.

Using the XO-121 type combustion chamber, a modified Super 88 engine was tested at various compression ratios and the results compared to those obtained for the XO-121. It became evident that there were many areas requiring further development, including combustion chamber configuration, spark plug location, manifolding, camshaft and valve timing.

A series of tests were conducted, taking one item at a time. Evaluation and comparison of the results of these tests constituted a well-integrated, long-range development program. Results of this long-range program were very rewarding, as evidenced by the Nebraska test results of the Oliver 1800 tractor with this new gasoline engine.

Development Of Oliver's New Gasoline Engine

Agriculture continues to progress each year through new techniques and improved mechanization. The farm tractor industry is contributing much to this advancement by providing more efficient engines. In part, such engines have been made possible by the continuing improvement in the quality of petroleum products. The ultimate objective, of course, is to provide the farmer with the lowest overall equipment costs.

In the interest of providing our customers with the most efficient engine for best utilization of available fuels, Oliver has carried out an active engine research program since the early 1900s. The introduction in 1935 of the Oliver 70 tractor, with its high compression six-cylinder engine, represented a milestone for utilization of fuel qualities then available. Further research continued, and in 1954 Oliver announced the results of tests on the XO-121 engine through the ASAE paper, "Looking Ahead of Tomorrow in Tractor Engine Design" by T.H. Morrell and H.K. Dommel.

The XO-121 was an experimental four-cylinder overhead-valve engine, with a bore of 3-3/4 inches and stroke of 4-1/2 inches providing 100 cubic-inch displacement. This engine derived its name from its 12:1 compression ratio. At this ratio, experimental gasoline with octane rating considerable higher than that commercially available was required. Designed as a research engine only, the XO-121 illustrated the performance improvements which could be achieved through use of improved fuels permitting higher compression ratios.

The performance of this engine was exceptional and fuel economy was especially gratifying. An observed fuel consumption of 0.400 lb/hp/hour was obtained at the flywheel with accessories. When installed in a tractor, fuel consumption of 0.400 lb/hp/hour was recorded on belt pulley power tests.

The paper by H. T. Mueller and R. E. Gish of Ethyl Corporation presented at the September 1954 SAE meeting and entitled, "Tractor Engine Design Requirements for Best Fuel Utilization" contained the results of an additional study conducted by Ethyl Corporation of the XO-121 at compression of 7.0 and 9.5:1. The purpose of this investigation was to relate the performance of the XO-121 engine at lower ratios and lower fuel quality to that of production engines then available. These studies proved that substantial gains in performance could be obtained by applying the XO-121 principles to present-day engines.

To apply the concepts of the XO-121 to a production engine, we selected our basic Super 88 gasoline engine for further development in 1955. This was a six cylinder, 3-3/4-inch bore by 4-inch stroke, 265 cubic-inch, valve-in-head, wet-sleeve engine with 7.0:1 compression ratio. This paper covers the steps and considerations involved in the development of Oliver's new 1800 gasoline engines from this 1955 beginning.

Two-Piece Cylinder Head

For our development work, we decided to apply a new cylinder head of two-piece construction with an XO-type combustion chamber to the Super 88 engine. We had been experimenting for some time with two-cylinder head designs and had accumulated considerable field experience with several hundred two-piece heads on the Super 88 and other models. This development was originated by G.W. Bird, our former plant manager, who is now retired.

The design consists of a main lower cylinder head casting with a separate cover casting, as shown in Figure 1. The mating surfaces of the head body and cover are first machined, then assembled with a gasket between them. The remainder of the machining is accomplished as if the head was of one-piece construction. The benefits derived from such a design are:

1. Easier to cast.
2. Reduced dry sand core weight.
3. Reduced casting scrap from core shift or blow holes.
4. Easier to clean.
5. Elimination of cooling restrictions by removing all fins, core wires and core sand.
6. Easier to inspect and determine if casting is sound prior to machining.

The adaptation of the two-piece construction is desirable for more consistent cooling to permit maximum performance from a high-compression engine.

Compression Ratio Study

The first step in the development of this new engine was to evaluate the performance of the XO-type combustion chamber at various compression ratios and compare this performance to the yardstick previously established by the XO-121 engine studies. To accomplish this, cylinder heads were provided with compression ratios of 7.0, 8.0, 9.5, and 12.0:1. Figures 2 and 3 show cross sections of the 7:1 and 12:1 cylinder heads. Intermediate compression ratios were obtained by varying the depth of combustion chamber. The 18-mm spark plugs were located on the left side of the engine between external (non-water jacketed) exhaust ports. The valves and roof of the chamber were placed at a 12 degree angle.

Figure 4 shows the performance of this engine with the XO-type head at various compression ratios and the performance of the XO-121 at the same ratios. To eliminate the

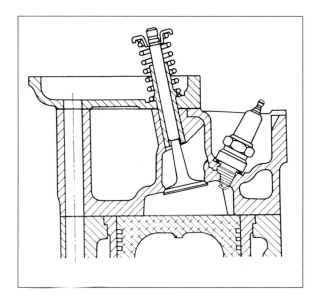

Figure 2: The 7.0:1 compression ratio head configuration. *Society of Automotive Engineers*

Figure 3: The 12.0:1 compression ratio head configuration. *Society of Automotive Engineers*

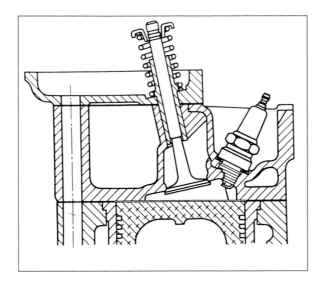

Figure 4: Performance comparison of the XO-121 engine with the Super 88 engine at 1,600 rpm without a fan. *Society of Automotive Engineers*

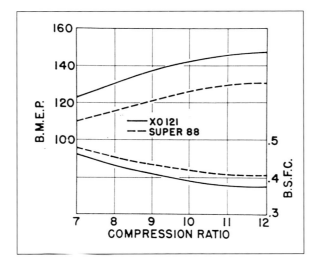

adverse effect of detonation on performance, special non-knocking high-octane fuel was used for this comparison. Although the Super 88 showed acceptable performance at the various ratios and response to changes in ratio, the results were not as good as our previously established XO-121 "yardstick". This is noted by the higher brake mean effective pressure and lower specific fuel consumption of the XO-121 at each compression ratio. These results illustrate that design principles employed on one engine do not necessarily hold true on another engine with a different design configuration. It became evident that additional refinement would be required to secure peak performance.

This further development of the Super 88 engine was resolved into the following phases for additional studies:

1. Structural rigidity.
2. Combustion chamber configuration.
3. Induction and exhaust system analysis.

Structural Rigidity

The results of some early tests indicated that performance might be improved by increasing structural rigidity. A prime factor in the structural rigidity studies was to provide our customer with increased engine life through great durability, in addition to improved efficiency and low cost of operation. Since we were carrying out a parallel future diesel program which might also benefit from increased structural rigidity, and considering operation at speeds faster than 1600 rpm, we decided to test and evaluate a crankshaft with seven main bearings as shown in Figure 5. At the same time, a full-pressure lubrication system with high-capacity gear pump was incorporated, replacing the metered system previously used.

Friction studies showed no noticeable difference between the engine with seven main bearings and the production engine with four main bearings. Any added friction of the three additional bearings could not be detected. At high speeds, power output was slightly improved and engine operation was somewhat smoother with the seven bearing engine. Thus, we decided to adopt the seven bearing design for our overall future engine program.

Combustion Chamber Configuration

The next step was to concentrate on combustion chamber configuration and to develop a high-ratio chamber which would provide maximum power and economy using regular gasoline. For this study, the 8.0:1 compression ratio head was selected.

We felt that performance could be improved by increasing the amount of turbulence in the chamber through improved "squish" action. There appeared to be a "dead area" at the shallow end of the chamber, especially at lower compression ratios. The first attempt to correct this problem was to bevel the back wall of the chamber at a 45 degree angle, as shown in Figure 6. The results of this modification were disappointing and indicated a performance loss of approximately two horsepower, apparently due to a reduction in the "squish" area.

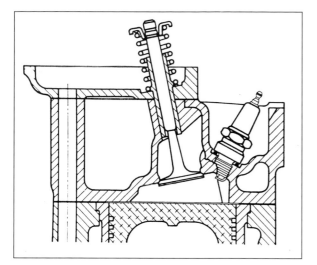

Figure 6: The beveled back combustion chamber with 8.0:1 compression ratio. *Society of Automotive Engineers*

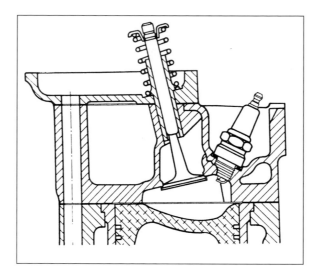

Squish height (distance from piston to cylinder head) was also investigated and the optimum height was determined to be 0.040 to 0.060 inches. The squish path was very important to concentrate the fuel-air mixture in the spark plug area. When spark plugs were evaluated, the projected-nose type was found to provide a slightly flatter spark traverse curve with better power at retarded spark settings. These results held true in additional developments.

The next attempt to improve turbulence was to reduce the depth of the combustion chamber by using the 9.5:1 ratio cylinder head and placing the remainder of the combustion chamber volume in the piston to obtain an overall ratio of 8.0:1. This combination is shown in Figure 7. The design, called the "concave piston," provided a more compact chamber, locating the spark plug closer to the squish path.

Cooling was improved in this step, as compared to the designs shown in Figures 2, 3 and 6. The compression rings were changed to a deeper section and moved down so that the top ring did not traverse above the water jacket. This reduced the temperatures in the ring belt, thereby providing longer ring and piston life.

Another combustion chamber configuration called the "wedge or hump piston" was also tested at 8.0:1 ratio. As shown in Figure 8, this consisted in machining the roof of the combustion chamber and providing a matching wedge or hump on the top of the piston. A por-

tion of the combustion chamber volume was provided by lowering the flat deck of the piston approximately 3/16" below the top of the sleeve. We believed that this design, while still retaining a compact chamber, might improve performance by directing the squish directly past the valves to the spark plug and thus creating better turbulence and scavenging in the spark plug area.

To fully evaluate the performance of these chambers with fuels of different octane ratings for comparison with flat-piston design, the "knock-rating" procedure previously developed by Ethyl Corporation was employed. Basically, this procedure involves the following three steps:

1. Running a series of spark traverse curves at various speeds using a special high-octane development fuel to prevent knock. The development fuel is

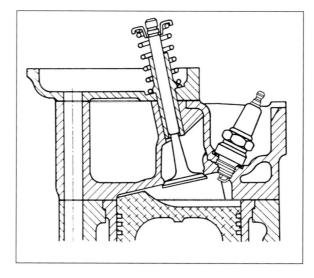

Figure 8: The wedge piston design. *Society of Automotive Engineers*

similar to a regular-grade gasoline in all respects except octane number. The carburetor is adjusted to deliver the final calibration air-fuel ratio at each speed. The runs provide power and specific fuel consumption data for spark timings ranging from greatly retarded to beyond maximum power without interference from knock.

2. Determining knock-limited spark timings at various speeds on two series of special full-boiling, commercial-type reference fuels. The fuels in one series have zero sensitivity, whereas those in the other have a sensitivity of ten. Motor octane numbers range from 72 to 87 in 5-octane increments in each series. Thus, the fuels range from 72 Motor-72 Research, to 87 Motor-97 Research. The knock-limited spark timing is that required to produce a barely audible knock (commonly called trace or borderline knock). The same air-fuel ratios used during spark traverse tests on development fuel are maintained during the knock tests.

3. Interpolating between reference fuels to determine spark timings for borderline knock on fuels of any desired octane number and sensitivity, and then finding the corresponding power and specific fuel consumption data from the spark traverse curves.

For our analysis of the three combustion chambers, we selected the following hypothetical fuels:

Low-80.5 Motor, 88.5 Research
Average-83.0 Motor, 91.5 Research
High-86.0 Motor, 95.0 Research

The borderline knock-limited performance of the three combustion chambers with these hypothetical fuels are shown on Figures 9, 10 and 11. In these tests, the "concave" piston design provided superior performance with all three fuels, indicating good fuel utilization regardless of fuel quality. Although the "wedge" piston did not perform well with low-quality fuel, its performance improved at a greater rate than that of the other chambers when higher quality fuels were used. Data was not taken at speeds above 2200 rpm, but the results indicated that the "wedge" piston might perform quite well at higher speeds.

Some trouble was encountered with the wedge pistons due to a hot spot at the top of the wedge. This hot spot, which caused pre-ignition, was reduced but not entirely eliminated by redesign of the underhead of the piston.

An evaluation of the data obtained to this point indicated a possibility of reverse "squish" between the piston and head underneath the spark plug. The reverse "squish" appeared to counteract the main "squish" from the other side of the piston, thereby reducing the turbulence in the spark plug area. To investigate this possibility, a new cylinder head was designed, as shown in Figure 12. In this design, the valves were placed at an 11 degree angle instead of 12 degrees to obtain better rocker arm action, and the combustion chamber was shifted toward the spark plug side. The spark plug remained on the left side of the

Figure 9: Borderline knock-limited torque with low hypothetical fuel and 8.0:1 compression ratio. *Society of Automotive Engineers*

Figure 10: Borderline knock-limited torque with average hypothetical fuel and 8.0:1 compression ratio. *Society of Automotive Engineers*

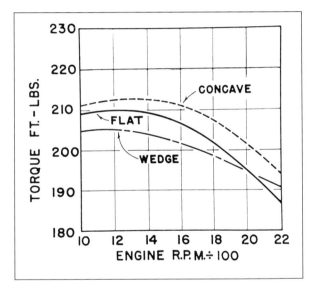

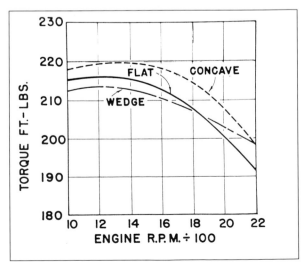

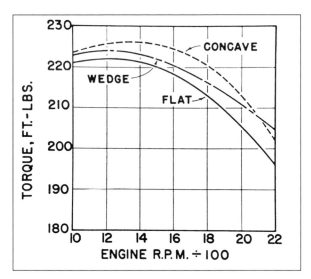

Figure 11: Borderline knock-limited torque with high hypothetical fuel and 8.0:1 compression ratio. *Society of Automotive Engineers*

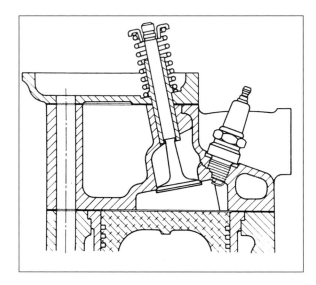

Figure 12: The revised head with 11° design. *Society of Automotive Engineers*

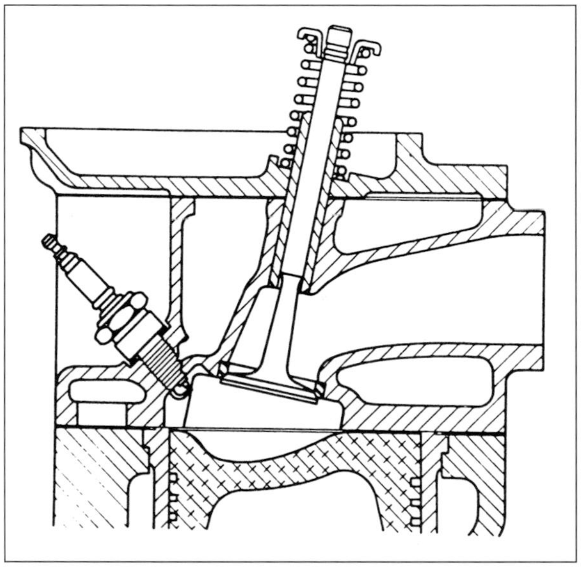

Figure 13: The final head and piston design used in the Model 1800 engine. *Society of Automotive Engineers*

engine between exposed (non-water jacketed) ports, but the ledge connecting the ports at the edge of the head was removed to prevent accumulation of dirt and trash around the spark plug. This head was tested with the flat piston and appeared equal to or slightly better than the previous flat-head piston designs.

It became evident at various stages of the development that spark plug life could be improved materially if the plugs could be moved away from the exhaust ports. Since the distributor was on the right side of the engine, it was desirable that the plugs be on the same side. Therefore, we decided to reverse the cylinder head and combustion chamber, placing the plugs on the right side while leaving the intake and exhaust ports on the left side of the engine, as shown in Figure 13. To further improve cooling around the spark plug it was necessary to decrease the plug size from 18 mm to 14 mm and use a 3/4" reach plug. The combustion chamber was shifted farther toward the spark plug side to eliminate reverse "squish" and to gain more "squish" area opposite the spark plug as can be seen in comparing Figures 7 and 13. Since the concave piston had continued to show improved fuel utilization over the wedge or flat-top pistons, all further development was continued with the concave design.

The name "Econo-Pak" was assigned to this final combustion chamber configuration. "Econo-Pak" was derived from the fuel economy capabilities of the compact combustion chamber.

Induction and Exhaust System Analysis

In anticipation of higher operating speeds and for better breathing, intake and exhaust valves and ports were enlarged. The reversed combustion chamber also permitted more streamlined intake and exhaust ports which reduced restriction of the intake air.

Studies of camshafts for higher speeds were made to determine if further improvements were possible. We evaluated a series of five different camshaft designs in which the lift and the opening and closing events were varied. The best camshaft design had the same timing as the original Super 88 but approximately 17% greater lift. The profiles of these two camshafts are compared in Figure 14. Figure 15 indicates considerable improvement in performance with the new high-lift camshaft throughout the speed range. To determine the necessary ramp design for this cam, a "Lashograph" was employed to determine lash loss under all conditions of operation. This was an optical device obtained from Ethyl Corporation which visually indicated valve lash during operation.

Manifold investigations were conducted throughout the entire development program, with various designs being tested. The original exhaust manifold connected to cylinder-head exhaust ports which were not water jacketed presented a warpage problem which was reduced by reversing the head and jacketing the exhaust ports. Further improvements in the exhaust manifold were made by using a special high-strength low-growth cast iron alloy, increasing the runner

size by 25%, and providing ribbing, as shown in Figure 16.

The intake-manifold investigation involved determination of riser and runner size, manifold shape, placement and amount of manifold heating and riser length. In the final design, heat was applied to the top of the "T" section above the riser, and a rectangular runner was employed to reduce any tendency for fuel to centrifuge out of the mixture. Individual porting of each cylinder was incorporated.

Final Performance

Following the completion of work on the induction system and related components, a borderline knock-rating analysis was again employed to determine the maximum compression ratio at which the engine could be operated when placed in production. For this analysis, typical 1961 fuels with octane ratings as follows were selected:

Low-82.5 Motor, 90.5 Research
Average-84.0 Motor, 92.5 Research
High-85.5 Motor, 94.5 Research

With these fuels, it was found that the engine developed maximum knock-limited power at a compression ratio of 8.5:1. This ratio was therefore selected for production. Figure 17 shows the performance of the Oliver 1800 engine at borderline knock with these three typical fuels.

A comparison of final performance of the Oliver 1800 gasoline engine as released for production with the original XO-121 engine and the Super 88 with XO-type combustion chamber, all at 8.5:1 compression ratio, is shown in Figure 18. These curves indicate the performance improvements obtained by the additional development of this engine and show that the performance goals established by the XO-121 at the same ratio can be obtained on a production engine.

One of the main objectives of this long-range research program was to maintain good economy throughout the complete operating speed range of the engine. The results were very gratifying, as evidenced by the relatively flat fuel economy curve in the speed range of 1000 to 2200 rpm.

The research program also permitted improvements in our Diesel engines which were derived from the two-piece cylinder head

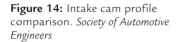

Figure 14: Intake cam profile comparison. *Society of Automotive Engineers*

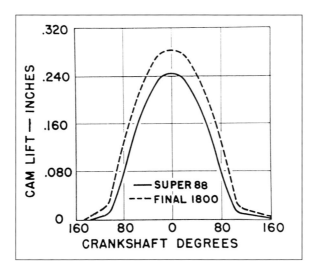

Figure 15: Camshaft performance with non-knocking fuel and 14:1 A.F.R. *Society of Automotive Engineers*

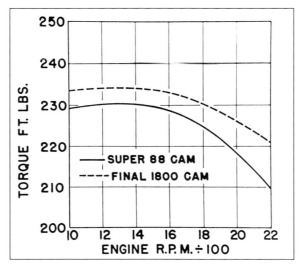

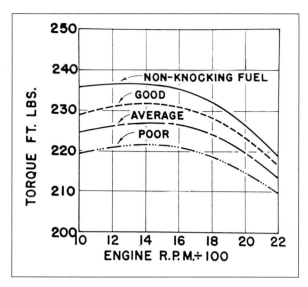

Figure 17: Borderline knock-limited torque with anticipated 1961 regular grade fuels and 8.5:1 compression ratio. *Society of Automotive Engineers*

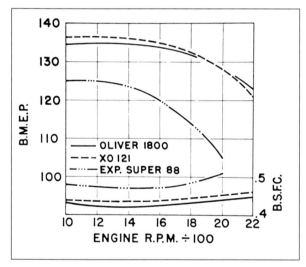

Figure 18: Final performance comparison with standard accessories. *Society of Automotive Engineers*

and studies of manifolding, and camshaft timing and profile, valve lash, lubrication and other design characteristics of a minor nature.

On Nebraska Test #766, the Model 1800 established a new all-time fuel economy record of 0.472 lb/hp-hour or 13.18 hp-hr/gal. on the maximum-power PTO test. Under the current test procedure, instituted in 1959, the following fuel economies were obtained:

These records were established despite a governed speed of 2000 rpm with power consuming accessories such as power steering and hydraulic pumps.

In conclusion, we can say that the results of this program have been very rewarding and have enabled us to provide an efficient reliable product for our customer.

Test Description	Lb/hp-hr	Hp-hr/gal.
Max. Power - PTO	0.472*	13.18*
Varying Power - PTO		
Rated	0.481*	12.93*
1/2 Rated	0.651*	9.56*
Maximum	0.474	13.14*
1/4 Rated	0.971*	6.41*
3/4 Rated	0.527*	11.80*
Average	0.590*	10.55*
Max. Drawbar Power	0.532*	11.70*
75% Pull Drawbar	0.566	10.99*
50% Pull Drawbar	0.688	9.04*

* - Denotes new record for current test procedure established by Test #766.

REFERENCES

Gray, R. B. 1954. *The Agricultural Tractor: 1855–1950*. St. Joseph, Michigan: American Society of Agricultural Engineers.

Gregg, G. R. 1965. *Progress in Tractor Power from 1898*. Charles City, Iowa: Oliver Corporation. (Reprinted by Alan King in 1976).

Gregg, G. R. 1975. *Field Boss*. Form R.1673. Charles City, Iowa: White Farm Equipment.

Hart-Parr 1912. *Catalog #13*. Charles City, Iowa: Hart-Parr. (Reprinted by Alan King).

Janssen, John E. 1996. *Hart-Parr Tractor's Contribution to the Advancement of Agriculture*. New York: American Society of Mechanical Engineers.

King, Alan. 1990. *Oliver Hart-Parr 1898–1975, Data Book No. 4*. Delaware, Ohio: Independent Print Shop.

King, Alan. 1981. *An Advertising History 1929 to 1940*. Radnor, Ohio: Alan King.

Letourneau, P. A. 1993. *Oliver Tractors: Photo Archive*. Minneapolis: Iconografix.

Pripps, Robert N, and Andrew Morland. 1994. *Oliver Tractors*. Osceola, Wisconsin: Motorbooks International.

Schaefer, Sherry, ed. *The Hart-Parr/Oliver Collector*. Charles City: The Hart-Parr/Oliver Collectors Association, P.O. Box 685, Charles City, Iowa 50616.

Van Syoc, Wendell M., ed. 1980. *An Historical Perspective of Farm Machinery*. Warrendale, Pennsylvania: Society of Automotive Engineers.

Wendel, C. H. 1993. *Oliver Hart-Parr*. Osceola, Wisconsin: Motorbooks International.

INDEX

PHOTO INDEX